I0475034

Swing Trading

A Beginners Guide to Swing Trades - Create Passive Income, Trading Tools, Money Management, Routines and Rules

Carl Hitoshi

Table of contents

INTRODUCTION

The "Swing Trading: A Beginner's Guide to Swing Trades - Create Passive Income, Trading Tools, Money Management, Routines and Rules" offers an introduction to the world of trading.

This book will help you to understand how to make your first trade, which tools you need to make a profit, and how to fit your strategies with your daily routine, plus more.

It's perfect for beginners that would learn how to trade, also for traders that would discovery new strategy to make big profits.

Swing trading is a particularly profitable type of approach, that allows to make first moneys outside your work.

If you do professional trading, you can do huge things but you need the basics to operate in markets. This book is for you.

You will discover:

-What swing trading is

-How to improve your skills

-The platforms and tools you need to have to become a trader

-What money management is and why it is so important

-How much capital you will need for starting trading

-How to protect your capital from unexpected changes of

the market

-How to organize your trading day

MULTIPLE TIME FRAME FOR SWING TRADING

Swing trading by itself is the most effective trading style that traders have available at their disposal. Swing traders make their money by taking chunks of swings that price makes as it moves up and down in the market. They are typically trend traders and the majority only trade in the direction of the major trend. This is the key to why and how swing traders typically outperform all other kinds of traders. However, there are a few ways that you can make or fine so that it produces even better results. One way that you can push this style of trading to the edge and give yourself an even larger edge over all other market players is by trading with multiple timeframes. This allows you to fine tune your entries and exits to potentially maximizing the returns on each trade you place.

Just how can you use swing trading and multiple timeframes to increase your trading edge? The first step is to make sure you pick the right kind before you even begin trading. Using different ones is only effective when the two timeframes you pick are compatible. Just what does it mean? One timeframe should be the overall or trend timeframe and the second timeframe is smaller than the first. These two timeframes must not be too close and yet at the same time, they shouldn't be too far apart. A good example of this and how it won't help you with your trading are the four hour and 15-minute timeframe. These two timeframes are too far apart to give you any kind of trading edge. Likewise, using the daily and 12 hours

timeframe is too close to be of any use. The two timeframes must be just right. This includes using the daily with the four-hour chart or the four hour with the hourly chart. These are considered by many traders to be most suitable timeframes for using several timeframes when trading.

Once you've decided on the timeframes, you need to understand how they are used. The larger timeframe is used for trend or market observation. This is the timeframe you mostly use. You observe the market, look for changes in trends and make decisions on where to enter and exit based from this larger timeframe. Just what is the smaller timeframe used for then? The answer is simple: entries and exits. When you have decided that a possible market setup is approaching, you switch to your smaller timeframe and basically try to fine tune your entry. The smaller timeframe allows you to view with greater detail the current state the market is in. If you are looking to go long, you may be able to use the smaller timeframe to time your entry once you have decided that any retracements or selling movement is gone and the market is getting ready to go up or long. The same can be performed when you have a trade open and you have decided it is time to get out of the market. The smaller timeframe may allow you to pinpoint, with more accuracy, the best time to close a trade.

Swing trading with multiple timeframes isn't necessary but when done properly, it can give any trader better market odds. The most important thing when using multiple timeframes is that you pick two timeframes that are compatible. They must not be too far apart and at the same time not too close. Picking timeframes that are too

close or far apart will not help you with your swing trading and will most likely only increase the number of losing trades.

RISK INVOLVED IN SWING TRADING

Swing trading is generally defined as a commodity, index or stock trading practices where the instruments are either sold or bought at or near the closure of either up or down price levels in swing trading that is caused by daily, and sometimes weekly price excitability. A swing trade status is generally opened for a longer time than just a day but shorter than the trend that follows trade or purchase and holds the investment strategies. Swing traders actually engage in exploring alterations in an instrument's price level which are caused by fluctuations between its prices being invited up by positivism and alternatively sold down by the pessimism about a period of some days, weeks and even months.

A Prognostic market trading algorithm or the trading system is referred to as a calculable pair of the trading rules which utilizes either the fundamental analysis or the technical analysis and gives the output in entrance, exit and the stop loss trade points with prices.

The trading algorithms are actually utilized for day trading and also the long-term trading business. The investments in the research area of the trading algorithms and systems have skyrocketed certainly by the investment banking companies such as Goldman Sachs that spends millions on the trading algorithm research and also staffs in relation to the algorithm team much strongly on its desk for trading business.

Risks involved:
The swing trading is defined as the short-term investment business which trends only for few days or may extend up to a few weeks like 2-3 weeks but not more than that. Therefore people who are interested in long-term trading must not enter into this business.

The risk of the loss in this field actually increases in the sideways price movement or a trading range than the bear market or the bull market, which is clearly moving in a certain direction as of the incremental potential for the false positives and whipsaws. In the trending markets, either the bull market or the bear market, the momentum can actually carry the price of the traded instrument for a really longer than general time in single direction only. This makes the swing trading strategies which do not integrate this trending lesser beneficial than the trend that follows the strategies.

It is generally known to every person in trading business that all the fiscal instrumental risks of the loss in swing Forex trading is significant and just mitigated by the swing trading strategy. It is back examined and experimented on any certain commodity, index or equity and actually extends in order to prove all its worth, along with the successful and interesting trades all around.

IS INTRADAY SWING TRADING POSSIBLE?

This seems to be a question that comes up a lot. "Swing Trading" is typically defined as "a method or strategy used to profit from short-term (1-4 day) price moves in the market."

Although the standard definition defines the typical length of time in a trade (1-4 days), another definition for "Swing Trading" is used to describe a method or strategy used to profit from "price swings" in the market.

This definition can be used to define trading strategy or method, regardless of the timeframe used.

A "price swing" is used to describe the ebb and flow of price action.

As price moves from one point to the next, it typically does so in back and forth wave-like motions identified as "swings".

When price moves from a low point on a chart to a higher point, this is typically identified as an "upswing".

The opposite is true for a "downswing" in price.

When price moves from a high point to a lower point on a chart, this is called a "down-swing".

These alternating "swing" extremes are further identified as "swing highs" and "swing lows" once they begin to retrace from their highest or lowest point.

Technical Analysts use these "swings" to identify label trends in a security.

A series of "up swings" and "down swings" that create higher highs and higher lows is classically defined as an UP trend.

The opposite being true to identify and define a DOWN trend.

So now that we have the terminology and definitions out of the way, let's get back to the original question.

Using the second definition of a "Swing Trader", you can surely see how a day trader can trade the "price swings" in the market.

Our main strategy for overnight Swing Trading is based on locating strong or weak stocks (and sectors) in relation to the market and trading these stocks (and ETF's) based on the context of the overall market conditions.

When we trade the "price swings" intraday, we use the exact same strategy!

If the overall market is strong, we are scanning the entire market looking for the strongest stocks and sectors.

Once we locate these strong stocks (and ETF's). we then use technical analysis to identify the "price swings" in each particular stock and ETF.

We want to be in sync with the market, so if the overall market is strong and has made a run up (UP swing) and has now retraced (DOWN swing), we are looking for LOW RISK trade setups in the strongest stocks and ETF's.

That way, if the market decides to make another UP swing, we can enter into and hopefully profit from the next price swing (UP swing) in the stocks and ETF's that we have identified as being stronger than the market.

In a weak market, we do the exact opposite.

We locate the weakest stocks and ETF's and then try to identify the best opportunity to SHORT each "down swing" in these stocks as the overall market trades lower.

Although this article simply scratches the surface when it comes to "Intraday Swing Trading", rest assured that there are many strategies one could come up with to attempt to profit from the intraday "price swings" in the market

SWING TRADING

Swing trading is a trading style where a stock is held for a period ranging from a few days to 2 or 3 weeks. Beginners in the stock market usually employ this style, although intermediate and advanced traders may also gain from it. Swing trading depends on the weekly or monthly fluctuations in stock prices. Monitoring short-term variations in the market must trade in this style, because the trader must be quick to react. Traders employing swing trading do not depend on the fundamental value of stocks; rather they stress price patterns and short-term momentum.

Swing trading lies somewhere between day trading and trend trading. In day trading, the trader holds on to a stock for a time period ranging from a few minutes to few hours. However, he does not hold the stock for more than a day. A trend trader, on the other hand, analyzes the fundamental trend of the stock, and may hold it for weeks or months. Swing traders do not wait for the prices to reach rock bottom while purchasing or for the highest prices while selling. Instead, they capitalize on the short-term movements in the stock market. Persons involved in swing trading do not face competition from big traders.

A person seeking success through swing trading must learn to pick the right stocks. The right stocks usually include the ones belonging to blue-chip companies. These stocks tend to swing between extreme values. A swing trader follows a stock for a couple of days during the upward swing. During the stock's downward journey, the trader simply switches over to another rising stock. Swing trading is most

profitable when the markets are stable. It is during this period that the stocks display a general pattern of rising and declining within a time span of a few days. In more unstable markets, stocks do not exhibit any expected oscillating patterns. They are either in rising mode or in falling mode, with less fluctuation. When those are the market conditions, swing trading is not a profitable option.

SWING TRADING SYSTEMS

Swing trading systems capitalize on the oscillations experienced in the stock prices. In this style of trading, the returns on a stock can be gained in few days or within a week or two. Traders employing this style can leverage on the short-term stock movements without fearing any stiff competition from the big players in the market. Swing trading systems are best suited for the at-home or part time traders. These traders do not have enough time for constantly monitoring the stock prices like the day traders. They can only afford to watch over the market progress once in a day or week. They have to rely on the services of broker firms, who notify them about the price changes using email alerts and newsletters.

Large trading firms or agencies cannot trade their stocks at a rapid pace, owing to the bulk size of the holdings. They therefore do not adopt swing trading systems as their mainstay. Instead, they utilize the trading system occasionally to earn small amounts of profit. Day traders also shy away from this style of trading because of their tendency of not holding onto a stock for more than a day. They trade their stocks within minutes or hours. The part time traders and the newcomers in the market mostly prefer swing-trading systems. The low risks and quick returns form an attractive combination for these traders. Swing trading systems are best employed in a stable market. Here, the stock prices show a general pattern of variation, most of which can be predicted. Often these small variations are ignored by the day trader and the long-term investors. A swing trader on the other hand sees loads of opportunities. He/she trades on stocks having minor fluctuations. In case of a bullish or bearish market, the stock prices tend to move in a single direction- either up or down. They do not fluctuate. Swing trading systems therefore cannot be employed in such markets. In the stable market, the best bet for the swing trader is the blue-chip stocks. These are the stocks that are actively traded in most exchanges. Stocks of big companies normally show major variations, which translate into greater profits for the swing trader.

SWING TRADING STOCKS

Here are some of the differences between Swing Trading Stocks and Day Trading. Day Trading is called 'Day Trading' for the obvious reason that it relates to a particular span of time and Swing Trading Stocks also represents a particular span of time. The span of time that Swing Trading represents is a longer period of time than day trading but a shorter period of time than someone who is 'investing' or in for the long term. For accounting and tax purposes, anything less than a year is considered 'short-term' trading. Anything over a year is considered 'long-term'.

Swing trading is a different 'style' of trading. It suits individuals that would rather be in a trade longer than a day trader would. Day traders very seldom let a trade stay in effect overnight. They will enter a position and exit that same position on the same day. Swing traders will leave their trade open for a couple of weeks to as long as several months.

Swing Trading Stocks Pros and Cons

As with all things, Swing Trading Stocks has its good side & bad side

Those that swing trade stocks tend to believe that they are in a less vulnerable position than the positions held by day traders. Although one can understand their thought process, it is believed that they are both equally risky depending upon the experience, psychology and technical analysis technique employed by the trader. Everyone seems to think that long term investing is the safest bet but that is not always valid in view of recent statistics. In my opinion, the longer a trade is exposed to the markets, the more risk is evident. Investment brokerages have convinced the general public that investing is too complicated for the average guy and that he should leave his money with the brokerage for 'safe-keeping'.

The Pros of Swing Trading Stocks

- Less time consuming than day trading. A trader is given more time in between trades to perform his/her analysis and could possibly choose better performers.

- An initial poor entry has time to recover and return to a positive state dependent upon the direction the trader has chosen. Long (up) positions will often fair better in this respect than an initial Short (down) position.

- Swing Traders need not be concerned with meeting the 'Pattern Day Trader' requirements.

- Swing traders are given more data to analyze (timeframe wise) than are day traders. A swing trader has more confidence in his/her trade because the current trend is supported by longer term historical data.

The Cons of Swing Trading Stocks (double edged swords from the Pros listed above)

- Less time consuming than day trading. A trader is given more time in between trades to perform his/her analysis and could possibly choose better performers.

   Con: A Swing Trader can also get bad information into the mix of their data analysis and choose a less profitable performing stock or a losing stock.

- An initial poor entry has time to recover and return to a positive state dependent upon the direction the trader has chosen. Long (up) positions will often fair better in this respect than an initial Short (down) position.

   Con: An initial poor entry also has time to keep moving against your trade.

A swing trader, day trader or any 'trader' must be aware at all times of what they are doing and what they could expect from any given trade. Here is a brief checklist of very basic things to analyze before entering into a trade along with a little tip.

Check your confidence level on the following:

Psychology of the trade

Are you in control of your fear, greed, patience and desperation? Make sure your swing trading plan virtually eliminates any of these emotions, else you could make a hasty decision. Also make sure that you are trading only disposable capital to eliminate desperate decision making.

Up (Long) or Down (Short)

Any trade will return you to the very basic question that you must answer before entering the trade. Do you think the stock is going to go up or down? What analysis has brought you to this conclusion and do you have supporting evidence from outside sources for your answer? If you cannot give your answer some support, then your answer may be just a 'guess' and you might want to consider not entering the trade at all.

Confidence in your strategy

Are your technical indicators proven by YOU? Have you used them before by paper trading or with other trades? Have they worked for you? Simple Moving Averages and Exponential Moving Averages tend to be one of the most consistent technical indicators available.

DAY TRADING AND SWING TRADING

Day trading and swing trades have two things in common. Both styles of trading hope to make money from short moves in the market. They are not for the faint of heart. To offset the risk, of course, there is also the possibility of great returns! There is really nothing that compares to the excitement of completing a very successful trade. Some of these trades will last minutes and some as long as several days.

Day trading and swing trades are different in that swing trades are less flexible. Day trading proponents get out at the end of every day but are often doing multiple trades per day. One of the strengths of this is knowing where you stand at the close of each day. Swing trades may finish in a day or longer but are just as likely to last for a few days and during the course of a trade, there are more likely to be more ups and downs in profitability. There is potential to earn more from each swing trade, but there are risks. Day trading and swing trading may well be your ticket to quitting the day job if you so desire.

Day trading has no overnight risks, as long as all trades are closed before the market closes. Swing trades are more susceptible to news or economic climate during the trading day or at night. This news can have a negative effect on your position beyond the control of the swing trade system. Day trading or swing trading without a system will most likely be unprofitable.

Day trading or swing trading systems start at $2000 and go up from there. There is a lot of variety in the approach different traders take to develop a winning system. How you create your system for trading can be a real mix of philosophies, but the most important thing is to stick to your system. Up or down market direction makes no difference, as there are always big opportunities in day trading and swing trades in a variety of markets.

It is possible to trade a few stocks on a regular basis, as long as they follow your predetermined set of rules for trade signals. Trading the same list of stocks has the added incentive that you begin to get a feel for what a stock is likely to do when different news or economic factors occur. If you have a reliable stock pick resource to start with, it helps you to screen out the bad and find new stocks.

It's advisable to establish a system, for both the swing trades parameters and new stock picks, away from the emotion of the day trading process. A stock that does well with day trading may not do well with swing trading.

Comparing Day Trading and Swing Trading

Day trading means you open and close trades during the same day. The dominant consideration during day trading is the phenomenon of support and resistance. The phenomenon of daily trends plays a decisive role in day trading activities. Day trading is based on, chiefly, fizzling emotions of buyers and sellers. The linkage between bubble emotions (i.e., greed, fear, etc.) with investors' mindset (i.e., bull, bear, etc.,) creates situations for capital gain or loss.

The movement of a share price normally exhibits trends with repetitive swings. The phenomenon of swings creates an opportunity of capital gain, now and again. Swing

trading is an investment activity in financial markets where a tradable asset is held for between one to several days in an effort to profit from price changes or 'swings'. A swing trader does not place trades daily. Swing trading provides for a much larger profit potential than day trading. Swing trading requires more patience and understanding of stock market. Investors may hold the trade for a few days or weeks and it really depends on how well the stock trends/swings. Generally, a swing trader defines a satisfaction level about duration of swing but due to unexpected longevity or shortening of trend, it may increase his anxiety level or can disturb the comfort zone. These moments are critical, as a novice swing investor might take impatient decisions. Swing trading demands poised behavior and thorough research, fundamental and technical, of a share, company, industry and economy. A seasoned swing trader buys when people are selling and sell when people are buying through better understanding of forthcoming trends and swings, so that, he does not overreact to news, events and sentiments. He enjoys the riding of a trend until there are signs of reversal or retracement. Market experts define and suggest to swing traders, "Retracements are temporary price reversals that take place within a larger trend. The key here is that these price reversals are temporary, and do not indicate a change in the larger trend. Trend without retracement is unhealthy or dangerous trend. Since the definition of a trend is "a series of higher highs and higher lows," then logically speaking, the trend has to be over when the stock fails to establish a higher high and sets a lower low instead. A lower high is unhealthy, but it is not the end of the trend.

It is possible that after setting a lower high, the stock could retrace again, never setting a lower low, and then push above the previous high to a higher high. The nail in the coffin of a bullish trend is the establishment of the lower low. Once the lower low is in place, normally, trend is over. This is called a Reversal."

In day trading, the investor has small targets for profit. In swing trading, the investor has fairly big targets for profits. The realizations of targets depend on better understanding of trends and behavioral strength of investor towards market trends. An impatient/non-strategist loses money while a patient/strategist gains money. A tradeoff situation appears when the day trading target is apparently feasible but swing trading target is uncertain. The selection of one target is achieved at the cost of the other, i.e., the opportunity cost of day trading profit is swing trading profit or vice versa. A swing trader prefers dividend earning, so he acts proactively during book closure days of a company.

PROBLEMS WITH SWING TRADING USING OPTIONS

Swing trading is one of the most common ways of trading in the stock market. Whether you know it or not, you probably have been swing trading all these while. Swing trading is buying now and then selling a few days or weeks later when prices are higher or lower (in the case of a short). Such a price increase or decrease is known as a "Price Swing", hence the term "Swing Trading".

Most beginners to options trading take up options as a form of leverage for their swing trading. They want to buy call options when prices are low and then quickly sell them a few days or weeks later for a leveraged gain. Vice versa true for put options. However, many such beginners quickly found out the hard way that in options swing trading, they could still make a substantial loss even if the stock eventually did move in the direction that they predicted.

How is that so? What are some problems associated with swing trading using options that they failed to take note of?

Indeed, even though options can be used quite simply as leveraged substitution for trading the underlying stock, there are a few things about options that most beginners fail to take note of.

Strike Price
It doesn't take long for anyone to realize that there are many options available across many strike prices for all

optionable stocks. The obvious choice that beginners commonly make is to buy the "cheap" out of the money options for higher leverage. Out of the money options are options that have no built-in value in them. These are call options with strike prices higher than the prevailing stock price or put options with strike prices lower than the prevailing stock price.

The problem with buying out of the money options in swing trading is that even if the underlying stock move in the direction of your prediction (upwards for buying call options and downwards for buying put options), you could still lose ALL your money if the stock did not exceed the strike price of the options you bought! That's right, this is known as to "Expire Out of The Money" which makes all the options you bought worthless. This is also how most beginners lose all their money in options trading.

In general, the more out of the money the options are, the higher the leverage and the higher the risk that those options will expire worthless, losing you all the money put into them. The more in the money the options are, the lower more expensive they are due to the value built into them, the lower the leverage becomes but the lower the risk of expiring worthless. You need to take the expected magnitude of the move and the amount of risk you can take into consideration when deciding which strike price to buy for swing trading with options. If you expect a big move, out of the money options would of course give you tremendous rewards but if the move fails to exceed the strike price of those options by expiration, a nasty awakening awaits.

Expiration Date

Unlike swing trading with stocks which you can hold on to perpetually when things go wrong, options have a definite expiration date. This means that if you are wrong, you will very quickly lose money when expiration arrives without the benefit of being able to hold on to the position and wait for a return or dividend.

Swing trading with options is fighting against time. The faster the stock moves, the surer you are of profit. Good news is, all optionable stocks have options across many expiration months as well. Nearer month options are cheaper and further month options are more expensive. As such, if you are confident that the underlying stock is going to move quickly, you could trade with nearer expiration month options or what is called "Front Month Options", which are cheaper and therefore have a higher leverage. If you wish to give more time for the stock to move, you could choose a further expiration month which will of course be more expensive and therefore have a much lower leverage.

As such, the choice of expiration month for swing trading with options is largely a choice between leverage and time. Take note that you can sell profitable options way before their expiration dates. As such, most swing traders go for options with 2 to 3 months left to expiration at least.

Extrinsic Value

Extrinsic value or commonly known as "premium", is the part of the price of an option which goes away completely when expiration arrives. This is why out of the money options that is mentioned above expires worthless because their entire price consists only of extrinsic

32

value and no built-in value (intrinsic value).

The thing about extrinsic value is that it erodes under two conditions; by time and by volatility crunch. Eroding or extrinsic value over time as expiration approaches is known as "Time Decay". The longer you hold an option that is not profitable, the cheaper the option becomes and eventually it could become worthless. This is why swing trading with options is a race against time. The faster the stock you pick moves, the surer of profit you are. It is unlike swing trading with the stock itself where you make a profit as long as it moves eventually, no matter how long it takes.

Eroding of extrinsic value when the "excitement" or "anticipation" on the stock drops is known as a "Volatility Crunch". When a stock is expected to make a significant move by a definite time in the future like an earnings release or court verdict, implied volatility builds up and options on that stock becomes more and more expensive. The extra cost built up through anticipation of such events erodes completely once the event is announced and hits the wires. This is what volatility crunch is all about and why a lot of beginners to options trading attempting to swing trade a stock through its earnings release lose money. Yes, the extrinsic value erosion by volatility crunch can be so high that even if the stock did move powerfully in the predicted direction, you may not make any profit, as the price move has been priced into the extrinsic value itself.

As such, when swing trading with options, you need to consider a more complex strategy when speculating on high volatility stocks or events. You will therefore be able to choose stocks that move before the effects of time decay takes a big mouthful of that profit away.

Bid-Ask Spread

The bid-ask spread of options can be significantly larger than the bid-ask spread of their underlying stock if the options are not heavily traded. A large bid-ask spread introduces a huge upfront loss to the position especially for cheap out of the money options, putting you into a significant loss right from the start. As such, it is imperative in options trading to trade options with a tight bid-ask spread in order to ensure liquidity and a small upfront loss. Swing trading with options can be an extremely rewarding and profitable venture when you take all of the above issues into mind and choose your options wisely.

SHOULD I BE A SWING TRADER?

Do you want to play the stock market but feel it is just too intense for you? Or maybe you have a full-time job during the day and can't sit at your computer with a direct-access system ready with your finger on mouse button waiting to click. You need a trading style that doesn't leave you bound by your stocks and hanging around for the end of the trading day. What you need to look into is swing trading stocks to fit your situation and still allow the same excitement a trader can get from making those good trades.

Swing trading is a diverse style that is popular for many reasons. This trading style relies on strong uptrends or downtrends that allow the trader to swing on a chosen trend as long as it lasts. Swing traders base their stock trading decision on a lot of research done in between working and other daily responsibilities. So, swing trading stocks has the flexibility someone needs in a stock trading style. The research is needed for a deeper understanding of the stocks one is interested in investing in.

The stock research to be done is looking back at past trends, allowing you to come up with an informed decision on what to do. That way you can take a calculated risk of how long the trend will last in an uptrend or how short you need to go on a downtrend to maximize your profits. The use of end-of-the-day charts software and the information provided by your broker is also used to make your stock trading decisions. This eliminates the need of a direct-access system, being bound by your stocks and waiting for the end-of-the- day trading.

Most swing traders generally trade in blocks of 1000 shares at a time but this is more of a guideline then a rule. In addition, these traders will hold only 10 positions at a time. The type of stocks a swing trader will choose for their stock picks are those that can be moved quickly or at least in the near future. Below is a list of criteria used by the swing trader to analyze the stocks and decide on the stock picks.

Volume and Liquidity

Wanting stocks: they can move quickly and they work with actively traded and large stocks that are easier to trade.

Trending

This is the uptrend and downtrend mentioned previously. Stocks that are following these trend patterns rather than a straight one is what swing traders are looking for.

Volatility

Volatility of a stock is showing it has a lot of movement. Another criterion a swing trader looks for because the traders can profit quickly with a volatile stock.

Sector Selection

When stocks are in the strong sector, the swing trader finds it easier to trade but in the weak sector, profits are made by shorting a stock or the weakening price.

Tight Spreads

Tight spreads mean small spreads in the bid and the ask of a stock. Swing traders want the smaller spread because they can profit more from it. With a wider spread, a trader looks to have lower profits. So, the tighter the better.

Swing trading stocks is a diverse style of trading and fits well for anyone who has a full-time job and still wants to trade. It still involves a lot of work but at least it is more flexible to do your trading with. You just have to find the time to do the research needed for swing trading stock and you will be able to feel the excitement other traders feel after making a good trade.

THRILL OF SWING TRADING

Swing trading is basically a kind of stock trading. But the skill it requires is somewhat different from the normal methods. A well-disciplined approach towards the day to day happenings in each market is very necessary for a good swing trader because it is not a case where we can check for a chance, as we are putting the real money in it.

If you are not capable of taking risks, then swing trading won't be a good option for you. It is true that low reward low risk trading will be very safe way. But in the swing trading with increased risk, you can get good reward. The basic decision a swing trader should take is about when to enter and quit the market for making profit. For this, they cannot have any exact method or scientific way.

The swing trading strategy consists mainly of two activities: buying and selling of options, stocks, bonds, currencies, commodities etc. However, the process is getting complicated by considering the fact when should buy and sell these things. Swing traders can't fix a right time for the high profit through these accurate selling and buying timings. The aim should be to buy at the low prices and sell at the high price timings.

Swing trading is highly dependent on the matured behavior in the market. Swing traders are making profit or loss from the right or wrong decisions of other firms. If you can take advantage out of the wrong timings of the other traders, you can make high profit by acting at the correct point. However, you should be patient enough to wait for the apt timings without making hasty decisions. But sometimes

quickness will be needed to take advantage of the situation.

Taking the wise decision at the accurate time is very important. Swing trading is not about the moving with herds. One's loss is another's gain. So, the self-discipline, patience and analyzing capacity will be the favorable factors in this. Aim at maximizing the profit and minimizing the loss to the portfolios.

Another fact about swing trading is that the stock will be buying at the beginning of a trending stock and holding it. Then towards the end of this trend, the stock should be sold. So, the trading is basically according to the change in trends. The time period of this strategic movement may last from one week to a month. It will solely depend upon the trend and the swing trader. The experience will help the swing traders to set their timings more logically and accurately. Any way this will be a short period process.

As planning is very important in swing trading, the traders will usually take the help of the history of the companies before entering in to deals. As this is a short-term process, the buying and selling of stocks should be very quick. For this, the swing traders will prefer the stocks of heavy trading reputed companies in the market. So, it will make the entry and exit much quicker. They will make the purchases at the beginning of the boom of that particular stock then try to sell it before it returns to lower levels.

Before entering the swing trading, be confident of yourself, then make the best experience in stock trading. This will gain you a lot from the swing trading strategies. Set your plans and do a well-disciplined stock market trading.

SWING TRADING TIPS

Swing trading is one of the trading styles which is commonly implemented in speculative activity in financial markets such as bonds, commodity, foreign exchange, stock and stock index. Usually, this trading style requires that a swing trader holds his or her trading position for more than one trading day, commonly 2 to 5 trading days. Swing trading is popular in the trading world, as this trading style usually has a good risk and reward ratio; it means the probability to gain profit is bigger than the risk that may rise in each trade.

In general, swing trading aims for 100 pips profit probability. Profit potential can be gained from every market swing. A swing trader, especially in foreign exchange and stock index market, can go either long or short to take every opportunity. It also means within a trading week, when a market is volatile, a swing trader may come across several trading opportunities he or she can take.

Compared to scalping trading or day trading, obviously swing trading has fewer trading opportunities. However, as you can see here, if you implement this trading style, probably you will have more time to do your other activities as you do not have to keep your eyes on a market all the trading day. Of course, you will only get fewer opportunities but with high probability to win for each opportunity. It is your call to choose which trading style to apply. No trading style is perfect, there is always plus and minus.

Now, if you certainly want to give a try to swing trading, you can find some strategies from many resources available in the internet. You may find some books and any other educational materials on swing trading. You can visit and be a member of some trading forums as well. However, there are also some fraudulent people claiming themselves as swing trading gurus but actually, they just want you to buy their rubbish education materials. Just be careful of such people.

Fortunately, after getting some basic understanding and experience on swing trading, you can be a good swing trader as well. You can even come up with your own swing trading strategies. Many people enjoy the benefit of developing their own swing trading strategies as they are the only ones who know their trading character, need and style. Never quit to learn to be a good swing trader, although without a doubt it will take longer time to master swing trading excellently but in the end all of your efforts will pay out.

COMPARATIVE ANALYSIS BETWEEN DAY TRADING AND SWING TRADING

Stock Market

A stock market is a place where shares of companies are sold and bought. The very purpose of a stock market is to collect capital from investors for companies through selling ownership rights (i.e., shares) and in return, companies offer dividends against each share. Investors are ultimate owners of a company, so that the number of shares indicates ownership strength of a shareholder. With the passage of time, the phenomenon of frequent ownership changing of shares has emerged; it brings capital gain/loss. A share therefore brings dividend and capital gain or loss. Consequently, a stock market has two types of traders - investor and speculator. An investor considers dominant dividends while the speculator looks chiefly at capital gain or loss. An investor starts with fundamental factors while the speculator begins with technical factors. An investor makes moves with patience while the speculator exploits market sentiments. It is interesting to note that dividend and capital gain or loss exhibit trends and swings. Investor/speculator takes a risk on account of uncertain trends and swings; consequently, they realize benefits or incur a loss. Concisely, the stock market offers a way to transfer risky investments from people who do not want to bear risk to people who are willing to bear risk if they are sufficiently compensated for it; it is an act of risk sharing for a company's growth. In addition, whenever a shareholder researches the company fundamentals, he/she learns about the Organizational Behavior

(OB) of the company. The research effort enhances the business acumen of shareholders, a learning effect of the stock market. A knowledge worker must get some monetary benefits in share business.

Trend Phenomena in Stock Market

We live in a versatile universe. Anything of our cosmic economy, animate or inanimate, has constant portion, variable segment, repetitive content and evolutionary features, so that it exhibits a predictable behavior. For example, seasons are limited and follow a pattern; moreover, they are repetitive. On account of available seasonal data, a reasonably accurate prediction of the seasons' behavior is statistically possible. Human behavior has some definite personality dimensions owing to naturally endowed intelligences and instincts. The prominent intelligences are perceptual intelligences, emotional intelligences and execution intelligences, while, the major instincts are parental instinct, gregarious instinct, learning instinct, and sex instinct. The presence or absence of some intelligence/instinct content shapes countless human mindsets/behaviors such as fear, greed, haste, panic, love, hate, speculation and prudence. The economic behavior, e.g., demand of something, is outcome of multiple emotions and perceptions. The economic behavior, buying and selling of shares, is ascertained, quantitatively, through price/volume movement. The edifice of technical analysis is thus based on Revealed Preferences, i.e., the actual buying and selling of shares. In economics, the term "trend" refers to the sustained movement of price. In share market trends, volume works together with price action. The separation of chaotic behavior from trend movement of price/volume is a major concern of technical analysis. The better understanding of trends gives competitive advantage to traders, both investor and speculator.

A trend generally exhibits three durations, i.e., short-term, medium-term and long-term. Normally, traders consider a trend lasting from a few days to a few weeks a short-term trend, durations covering anywhere from a few weeks to a few months are considered medium-term and longer time periods are referred to as long-term trend.

The terms bull (up) and bear (down) market generally refer to cyclical gains or losses of 15% to 20% or more. Each up or down market cycle generally lasts from several months to a few years. Over 10 to 20-year periods, the stock market cycles exhibit multiple bull and bear markets. These longer term cycles are called "secular" bull and bear markets.

Whenever a trend changes its direction, it is called the turning point of that trend. A turning point is based on buyers/sellers' collective behaviors, both static and dynamic, so that it reveals some predictable features. Technically, the turning points indicate resistance or support prices. The resistance/support prices are the signs of the existence of static dimension of a collective mindset, while the change in resistance/support level is due to dynamic nature of collective human self. The static behavior of economic agents is the very basis of static economic analysis and the shifting behavior of economic agents indicates dynamism and demands a dynamic analysis for true understanding of economic behavior. Consequently, the static-comparative and dynamic analysis is used to ascertain changing economic variables. The prominent statistical tools for analysis are average, standard deviation and correlation.

Benefits of Trend Phenomena

It is said that trends are friends. Although the stock market has long-term trends, investors can also spot daily or weekly or monthly trends. Profits opportunities develop by the hour, and an astute trader who understands, know more grow more, can take advantage of these trends. Some short trends signal the beginning of longer term moves in the market. Investors/speculators who find these looming possibilities, can profit before everyone else figures out that a trend has begun.

A share has intrinsic as well as market value. The intrinsic value of a share is due to company fundamentals, while the market value is determined by demand and supply situation of a share at a given point of time. In the long run, the intrinsic value and market value of a share coincide with each other, but there is divergence between intrinsic value and market value during short and medium periods. A wise investor/smart speculator captures the opportunity of divergence of prices and realizes the profit or capital gain on investment.

The entry and exit are two distinct aspects of stock trading. The entry of a trader is the exit of another trader. The opposite risk-return approach of traders materializes an actual trade. The entering decision is more of an art than a science, and it tends to depend on the existing trading activity, market sentiments and personal risk-return assessment. The portfolio management and exiting, on the other hand, is dominantly a science rather than an art. The actual profit/loss is decisive at the time of exit.

IMPROVING SWING TRADING METHODS AND REDUCING RISKS INVOLVED

Those who wish to become swing traders must be dedicated to the trade, as a close watch must be kept on the oscillation of the trading instrument. This is most often done by teams of traders with similar interests as well to help each other benefit from the increase and profit. The value of a trading instrument, whether it is stock, index or commodities will always be on drop or raise. This makes it possible to track and determine whether or not it should be bought into, traded or liquidated. This often takes an immense amount of skills with the ability to create or read analysis reports and more.

Swing trading through technical or fundamental analysis is a very complicated but rewarding option. The ability to trade out the points in which it is perfect to enter into a new investment or exit completely out of it is essential. These abilities are needed to also properly assess where the stop loss points will be on the analysis to help prevent losses when the trading instrument must be sold at a certain price.

Trading algorithm research is also one of the better methods to use in swing trading. Some companies spend several millions of dollars to accurately map out the possibilities to invest in for the best profits based on older figures. This can be done with a predictive market trading algorithm which will often make use of technical or fundamental analysis information as well. This is very

useful in creating the proper control points in which to automate the purchase and sale decisions of the trading instruments.

Since the volatility of the market cannot be controlled, the proper interpretation of what is going to happen is important in swing trading. You simply do not buy at the highest price at a higher cost and sell at the lowest costs because they will not benefit the trader. Swing trading is the exact opposite of this notion and can be easily practiced with the proper vision of the market and the trade instrument involved.

Reducing the risks involved in the world of swing trading is not always successful, but there are ways to make trading safer. False positives are some of the worst culprits in swing trading, as it could cause the accidental sale or purchase of a trading instrument because of an implied increase in value. When the trend continues to follow in a single direction for a trade instrument, swing trading may not be profitable and a different trend following trade method would be more suitable to make better trading decisions. This helps to weed out the long trends that fall and keep those which rise up.

UNDERSTANDING SCANNING OF STOCKS IN SWING TRADING

It is not tough to make money from swing trading but it requires a lot of dedication and full effort to be able to pull good money out of it. Once you have decided the type of trades, then it has to be a good idea in order to get the feel to understand that the market is affected by which type of things for the week ahead. There are some things to look at;

1. Economic Calendar
2. Charts
3. Industry Groups

Scanning For Stocks!

Scanning is important in order to understand some potential trades in the market. Always remember that you have to look for the stocks that have actually pulled back into the action zone of the swing traders. Every swing trader is looking for the stocks that are:

1. In stage 2 or stage 4.
2. In the strong trends.
3. Have the relative strength or the weakness.
4. At the resistance or support level.

The stocks that are showing certain features can be used for shifting. You need to add them into your lookup list.

Trading Strategy!

The above specifications will give us the signal whether the swing trading is long or short. After doing this process, run all through the look up list in order to search out for the potential trades in the market. It may happen that the scan of the stocks you did on Sunday may not give you a good setup; therefore there is a need to do the scanning once again with the help of similar criteria as explained above.

After that, lookup for the certain entry into the stock market with the use of the candlestick patterns. Once you have entered into the trading business, just forget about the opinions, news and market. You just have to concentrate on to the chart trading. You need to make use of your exit strategy in order to make losses or profits. If you want to make money with swing trading. then you have to learn everything before you get into this field. I have spent some good years in research about it and I hope I will be able to make you understand some things that I gained from my experience.

WHY SWING TRADING IS FAVORABLE FOR BEGINNER TRADERS

As a beginner trader, you need to understand the different trading time frames available. There are actually 4 timeframes to choose from. The first one is the day trading, then the swing trading, intermediate trading and lastly, the long-term trading timeframe. But if you're a beginner trader, it is encouraging to choose the swing or intermediate trading timeframe.

In day trading, everything moves fast. Stock price moves fast and it fluctuates fast that it can make you cry. You will be bombarded with countless information that only an experienced and knowledgeable trader can handle well. Beginner traders will really find it very daunting and challenging. And because they don't know what to do, they may eventually lose money in their trades.

Here are the benefits of swing trading:

1. You give yourself time to adjust to trading: Trading needs practice and time to get used to. If you want to become a profitable trader, you need to adjust to how the market behaves. With the swing trading time frame, you have the opportunity to do exactly this.

2. Identify the overall trend: Day traders capitalize on the slightest fluctuation of the price movement to gain profits. On the other hand, swing traders wait for a trend to form before they actually get in a trend. This helps them secure their trades. In this time frame, you'll see the beauty of trends and reversals.

The stock market can be compared to traffic hours. Day trading happens during the rush hour when traffic is just tight. Everybody is busy taking care of their own business. Everything looks and sounds like one big mess. Swing trading, on the other hand, happens in between rush hours. You get to maneuver your car in different lanes without any hassle. Traffic is definitely tolerable. If you're just learning how to drive, which scenario do you prefer? Starting out as a swing trader or an intermediate trader is the best way to be inducted into trading. This is what I believe. Although I am not encouraging beginner traders to start as a day trader, you can still trade this timeframe though. However, never do so without proper training, education and guidance. If you really want to be a day trader, you need stock market education, experience and consistent guidance from a trading coach. In order to be a successful trader, you must never skip or reject these 3 factors I just mentioned.

Before you take day trading into serious consideration, try reading more about swing or intermediate trading first.

FIVE (5) TIPS FOR SUCCESSFUL SWING TRADING

Swing trading is a style of investing in which you try to exploit the natural oscillations of stocks. Often stocks travel within a specific range of prices over a period of time, allowing you to profit from these periodical ups and downs. Swing trades are usually held for a few days to a few weeks, so it's much easier than day trading. However, it doesn't require you to forget about the money you invested for years as live positional investments.

Swing trading can be a profitable business but it can also be a tricky one, so make sure that you follow the tips I provide in this article:

1. **Don't be a day trader in disguise** - A lot of people simply call themselves swing traders but practice day trading. If you're monitoring the markets constantly or going in and out of trades all the time, you're setting yourself up for a fall.

2. **Set your exit levels properly and stick to them** - Swing trading requires discipline. When you enter a trade, set your stop loss and take profit levels. These aren't up to any modifications due to hunches, unless the market data changes sufficiently to justify it. You need to work with your initial settings to avoid turning this into a job.

3. **Follow a strategy** - The best swing trading tip I can give you is to not follow tips but a sound strategy. You need to have a system down so you can trade efficiently as well as profitably. There are a number of strategies. Find one or

more which work (even if you need to take a course to learn them) and simply apply them again and again.

4. Be emotionless - This is the culmination of the previous 3 tips. To be a successful swing trader, you must act without emotions. Emotional mistakes are the worst things a trader can suffer. You must follow your logical strategy and eradicate worries and feelings as they will lead to mistakes.

5. A mentor - Finding a mentor who can teach you the ins and outs of swing trading techniques is a marvelous thing to have. A good mentor can save you a lot of time, money and frustration. He or she can also cut down your learning curve massively, so you're making more money faster.

SWING TRADINGINDICATORS

Swing trade indicators are an important thing to study if you are interested in swing trading and the substantial money that can be made in this industry.

First, it is important to define swing trading. Swing trading is typically defined as buying or selling a stock at the end of a severe up or down pricing swing, which is caused by market fluctuation and volatility. Normally, people hold the stocks longer than one day, for typically a couple of weeks or months at the most and get rid of the stocks in a typically shorter time than normal investment advice would recommend.

Swing traders do not fly by the seat of their pants though, and most use successful trading strategies or algorithms to make their decisions. These techniques are seen also with other kinds of trading, including the popular day trading.

Large companies are extremely interested in the swing trading strategies and are basing many of their investment decisions and training programs on swing trading. Obviously, there are a lot of risks involved with this type of trading, as it is based on indicators as opposed to research into the exact stock itself and its chances of success.

Swing trade indicators are programs invented by investors and people who study the markets closely which tell you when to buy and sell stocks. These indicators measure the strength of a trend and can tell you what you may want to invest in and with another indication on how strong that trend is, to help you decide if that purchase is right for you.

There are hundreds of websites and programs online that are dedicated to help you learn swing trading, so it is notdifficult to find what is right for you. It is a technique which is proven to work if you can get the right program down. However, it is hard to weed through the mess of options you have online.

BEST SWING TRADING INDICATORS FOR A TRADER

Finding the right swing trading indicator can sometimes be very difficult. Technical trading with indicators is possible and many traders around the world are able to make profits day in and day out thanks to the insight that trading indicators offer to those with the skills to use them. If you are just starting out, then the problem is that there are many indicators available. This makes it extremely difficult when deciding on what indicator you should use. This is where new traders need a little help in understanding that all indicators work. The secret to finding the best trading indicator lies not in finding the right indicator, but instead, in finding the right indicator for you and your trading style. Some of the most popular trading indicators include RSI, MACD, Stochastics and many, many more. All of these indicators and others can be used for trading. They will work on any market and any timeframe, even if you don't swing trade. Instead of searching for the best indicator, ask yourself what trading style you prefer and what you want or need from your indicator. Indicators often display different aspects of markets. Some are leading and warn of potential areas where the market may be overbought or oversold. Some indicators are moving average based and instead, they plot the average of price on the chart. If you know what you need from an indicator, then you can find and start experimenting with indicators of that kind. This will make finding the

right indicator for your trading style much easier and
faster.

When you are testing and playing with trading indicators, always keep in mind that no indicator is perfect. When used properly, an indicator can give you a trading advantage. Some new traders make the assumption that the more indicators you place on your chart, the better a trader you will be. This couldn't be any further from the truth. It is recommended that you use at most 3 indicators at one time. If you start using any more than this, you may find that your charts become cluttered and that trading decisions will become more difficult. It is common that one indicator conflicts with the signal of another that you are using at the same time. In this situation which trading indicator do you follow? Keep it simple. Never use more than 3 indicators at a time.

There are plenty of trading and swing trading indicators available. Finding the right or the best trading indicator might not be easy, but you can simplify the process by first deciding which type or what kind of information you want your technical indicator to tell you. Do you want to know when the market may be exhausted and readying to pullback? Do you instead prefer to use moving averages of price? Once you know what you want, it will be easy to test and play with indicators of that kind until you find the one that suits your style. Furthermore, always remember that more is not always better. Keep your trading indicators on your chart to a minimum. Using any more than 3 may actually make trading more difficult and this is something no trader should want.

The Best Indicator for a Ranging or Trending Market
In swing trading, it is very important for you to use the trending indicators for a trending stock or security and a

ranging indictor to a ranging stock or security. Before swing trading a stock or a security, you need to determine whether the stock or the security is trending or ranging. You need to do this right in order to make your swing trading a profitable success.

So, the first important question that you need to ask before swing trading is whether this market is trending or not. The easiest way to determine a trend in the market is to take a look at the security chart. If you see a series of higher highs and lower lows in the chart, you know there is a trend. If not, then it is ranging. In that case, you need to see clear support and resistance areas meaning the security prices clearly rises and falls between these two levels.

When you eyeball the security chart, you are not every sure. It is a subjective thing that depends on the time frame that you are using on the charts. Suppose you are eyeballing on the one-hour chart. The security may appear to be trending, however, when you try to eyeball it on a daily chart, the security may appear to be ranging. As a swing trader, you should only rely on the hourly and daily charts. Anything longer is only appropriate for position traders or buy and hold investors. Now, if you are satisfied with your eyeballing the charts, you can use an indicator that can tell you about the strength of the trend. The most popular indicator that shows whether the security is trending or ranging is the Average Directional Index (ADX). ADX actually measures the strength of the trend rather than its direction. It oscillates between the value of 0 and 100. The standard setting for ADX is 14 days period.

If the ADX is below 20, the security is in a trading range and if the ADX is above 30, the security is considered to be trending. Readings between 20 and 30 are mostly ambiguous. When the reading is between 20 and 30, if the

ADX is rising and above 20, you can take it as trending. And if ADX is falling and below 30 but above 20, you can take it as the security is in a trading range.

As long as you are not able to determine whether the security is trending or non-trending (ranging), you should avoid planning any sort of a swing trade or for that matter any trade at all. The onus is on you to determine whether the security is trending or non-trending. The best way is to use the ADX indicator!

SWING TRADING IN FOREX - THE MIDDLE PATH

Swing trading has been popular among traders because it combines some of the advantages of two popular strategies, while avoiding a few of their unfavorable aspects. Day trading or trading on shorter timeframes is popular because it allows traders a degree of confidence. Confidence that their losses will not reach large sizes due to the smaller-sized movements that must be managed in the course of a single trading day, in comparison to the months or weeks that must be taken into account in a long-term strategy.

The advantage of long-term trading is born of the fact that analysis is easier, risk/reward studies are performed with greater ease and a higher degree of clarity is possible while strategies are being formulated. Swing trading aims to combine these favorable aspects of the two approaches into a workable, medium-term strategy.

The term is used to imply that swing traders usually aim to profit from turning points, such as those that exist at the upper or lower limits of price ranges or the inflection points on trend lines that constitute favorable entry/exit points for long term strategies. Nonetheless, it is accepted generally that swing trading is most applicable to ranging markets. Tops and bottoms are very difficult to identify in trending markets, and the bounds of a range are often much more favorable for the strategies employed by swing traders.

A successful swing trader must know when to enter a trade and must be very discerning about his options in a typical market. Success in this strategy depends very much on the isolation of favorable market conditions and the foregoing of opportunities that are riskier than what is tolerable for the trader.

Typical patterns commonly exploited by swing traders include triangles of all kinds, Fibonacci patterns inside daily ranges, as well as many developing range formations inside an ongoing longer term trend. Since these patterns can be easily analyzed by technical tools, a swing trader needs to establish the risk limits that are to be deemed acceptable, while the eventual direction of the price action remains inconsequential. In the same sense, the swing trader will immediately end his trading activity inside a previously convenient price formation once the range bounds confining the price action break down.

TO BUY AND HOLD OR SWING TRADE

You know the old saying: A stock analyst is someone who will know tomorrow why his predictions yesterday didn't happen today! And do you know why God created stock analysis? To make the local weather forecasters look good. Figuring out how to trade in the stock market is a skill everyone needs to learn. You need to understand when to get in and when to jump ship. Being flexible, decided and great at analysis, will help you take control of your stock portfolio.

A good stock trading method or strategy for these days is to learn how to swing trade. I don't think the buy and hold strategy works as well as it used to. This sounds straightforward, yet it is astonishing how many traders will buy stocks when the market is trending down and just hold on until they have loss a pile of money. A better idea I think, is to look for stocks that are trending up and buy the dips. This simple swing trading strategy is vital for success in today's markets.

You need to make the stock market just one of your many assets. Rather than only purchasing stocks and bonds, broadening the sort of investments you will be making allows you to have better likelihood of making money. Purchase real estate and look at gold and silver so you have the opportunity to profit if your stock portfolio starts to die.

Do not put all your eggs in one basket. It is always better to diversify. Also, once you enter a trade make sure you enter stop loss orders in the event the trade goes south. It is usually a good idea to policy to be prepared for the worst while you expect the best.

Analyze your stock portfolio meticulously. When you enter a new trade or liquidate a position, be sure that your trade has been entered correctly into your trading account. Mistakes do happen, so if you find an error, speak to the brokerage right away to get it corrected.

Remember that the price of stocks are always changing. So if you think that stock prices will remain where they are for quite a while or continue to trend higher you might be completely wrong, and you will lose money using this mindset. You must be flexible to make changes to your portfolio and exit the trades that are not working.

Before even buying your first stock, make sure you know your current total financial situation. What are your debts and income? Do you have six months reserve fund saved up? This should be done before buying a single share. Once it is accomplished, then you can determine how much of your income can you put towards stock trading? Once you know this, then determine your stock portfolio and watch it like a hawk.

Do your homework, but do not rely on just your knowledge. Informed decisions do come from research and doing your own leg work. Read, study and learn how to swing trade. However, financial experts and advisors do exist because they have already learned a lot, too. By relying on both them and yourself, you are getting the best of both worlds for the best possible position to make investment choices.

Before you start swing trading, it is a good idea to practice with a demo account. Choose several stocks and note the price and the date. Keep track of these picks and evaluate your reasons for wanting to invest. As you watch the charts

over time, you will develop insight into how effective your ability to pick a good stock is developing.

Spread out your money. You want your portfolio to be set up to weather losses. If all of your money is allocated to one stock or even one sector of the market, a single downturn could wipe you out. Manage your money effectively and you won't be as hurt by bad trades.

TAKING THE BEST FROM TREND TRADING AND SWING TRADING

Trend trading is a trading approach that offers the potential to reap greater profits by capitalizing on large market moves. There are two main concerns dealing with trend trading; either the market is trending upwards (bull trend) or trending downwards (bear trend). For the trend trader to profit, it is important to correctly identify the trend before a trade is placed.

When it comes to trend trading, once the trade has been placed, the trend trader will usually stay in the trade until such time that it appears the overall trend has changed.

Trends occur at different timeframes and can be seen on various time-frame charts. A trend trader, being more a long-term trader where trades usually last a few weeks or more, will likely define a trend from analyzing a daily or greater time-frame chart. Minute charts may be used for fine-tuning entry, they certainly would not be used for determining the trend.

The timeframe of the charts used is very important to the trend trader. If the trend is being defined on a weekly chart, it is the weekly chart that should be used to determine when the trend has ended as well. By doing this, the trader is not exiting a weekly or greater trend just because the trend has changed on the lower timeframe daily chart.

There are many counter-trend moves that occur within a complete trend move. These are usually seen on the lower timeframe charts in respects the timeframe used to define the trend. For example, if a weekly chart is used to define a bull trend in the SP500 market, there will be moves against this bull trend that will be easy to see on a daily time-frame chart. The trend trader would normally stay in a trade even when the market is moving against the position, as it is expected to recover soon if the trend is still intact.

Trend traders often use indicators such as the moving averages to determine when to enter and when to exit. For example, a trend trader may buy when the 50-day moving average is greater than the 200-day moving average and sell when the 50-day moves below.

For most traders, staying in a trade when the market is making a move against the trend direction is difficult to do. You really have to stick to your guns and avoid reacting to the market as it moves to erode your accumulated profits if you want to be successful as a strict trend trader.

The other type of trader to consider is the Swing Trader. Swing traders usually trade off the daily time-frame or lower (minute charts). Swing trading is all about following the market's most likely current direction. For new traders, swing trading can be a more effective approach due to the shorter period of holding a trade and usually less exposed in risk capital. Swing trading is considered by many to be an easier and less stressful way to enter the markets.

The swing trader will usually go long when the short-term market is confirming a swing bottom and looking to move up and going short when the market is confirming a swing top and looking to move down. Thus, while the trend trader may be holding a long based on a bullish weekly trend, the swing trader could be either long or short during this same period because of the direction the market is currently moving in the lower timeframe.

With trend trading, the cons are clear. You must allow for possible large moves against your position when the trend is in a counter-trend phase. With swing trading, the cons are also clear. While the overall market is trending in one direction, the swing trader will at times be trading against this trend which is often wrought with greater risk than trading with the overall trend.

Therefore, when considering the negative aspects of both trend trading and swing trading, why not simply use the best of both?

In order to do that, it is important to determine first the overall trend direction much like the trend trader would do. So, if you do so based on moving averages as in the earlier mentioned example, then all your trades should only be in that direction. Therefore, if the trend happens to be bullish, take long trades off swing bottoms and look to exit off swing tops rather than shorting them.

First, identify the current weekly trend based on the most recent formation of a weekly swing top or bottom in relation to previous weekly swings. Once the direction is determined, look to only enter the market while going 'with the trend'.

While swing traders will usually apply two or more indicators in an attempt to determine when the short-term swing is occurring, it is advisable to use mathematically calculated 'turn dates' that provide the date as to when these swings are most likely to occur. Once this is known, simply allow the market to confirm the swing which signals the trade entry.

Note these words found on page 11 of the book "How to

Make Profits Trading Commodities" by W. D. Gann.

"THE BEST WAY TO TRADE: The most money is made by swing trading or in long pull trades, that is following a definite trend as long as the trend is up or down...Wait for definite indications that it is going higher or lower, before you take a position for a long pull trade...get out when you get a definite indication that the market has reached a turning point and that the trend is changing."

So, in order to get the most of your trading and to keep your risk as low as possible, look to determine the overall trend first and then only trade off swings in that direction.

SWING TRADING STRATEGIES

Having a deep comprehension and apprehension of the swing trading strategies is the key to succeed in the haze of swing trading. Why? Because a firm grasp of those trading strategies allows swing traders to uncover new opportunities and time their entries and exits appropriately.

Swing trading strategies are not actually different of those used in options trading or forex trading; swing traders rely heavily on two main strategies: technical analysis and fundamental analysis. Swing traders, however, primarily use the technical analysis approach either solely or in conjunction with fundamental analysis.

Most day trader experts encourage to use both strategies as one complements the other. Indeed, technical analysis allows the trader to understand which stocks are moving while fundamental analysis will tell which stocks are likely to move.

Technical Analysis

Basically, swing traders using the technical analysis approach examine any financial instrument in a very short time horizon and base their decisions on its likely short-term direction.

Unlike those using the fundamental analysis approach -- more on that later -- technical analysts don't bother to catch up with corporate events (takeovers, acquisitions, etc.) and aren't concerned with earnings or valuation. Instead, they use charts along with other technical indicators on which their entry and exit decisions are based upon.

Fundamental Analysis

What's the company value compared to its peer? What's its growth rate, positive or negative? What is its return on investments?

These are questions fundamental analysts are constantly asking. These questions are quite different compared to those we can find in the technical approach.

Fundamental analysis strategy allows the trader to get an idea of how wealthy the company actually is and what price its share should reasonably trade at. For example, the higher the company's earnings are, the more traders will pay for a part of that company.

Which one to choose?

As said earlier, it's recommended to use both approaches as they complement each other. However, if you happen to only choose one strategy, it's important to be aware of its advantages and disadvantages.

The technical analysis strategy has one main advantage: it allows to uncover the underlying cracks of a company. While the fundamental analyst follows the trends on the surface, the technical analyst follows the trends under the surface of a company, which often left him in the minority -- which is an advantage in itself. One drawback of the technical analysis strategy is that since it is in large part of following indicators and whipsaws, therefore it might occasionally give cranky signals that might change a short while after. For that reason, you'll never know whether or not a chart pattern or indicator actually gives you an erroneous signal.

On the other hand, most of the time fundamental analysis can't give an accurate short-term point of view when you most need it. Also, fundamental analysis relies in large part on subjectivity and your capacity to interpret relevant market information. One advantage is that fundamental analysis leads to long-term profits since fundamentals drive the prices of financial instruments.

BENEFITS OF SWING TRADING

The process of swing trading has become a very popular stock trading strategy used by many traders across the market. This style of trading has proven to be very successful for many committed stocks and Forex traders. Traditionally, swing trading has been defined as a more speculative strategy as the positions are traditionally bought and held for the traders predetermined timeframe. These timeframes could range anywhere from two days to a few months. The goal of the swing trader is to identify the trend, either up or down and place their trades in the most advantageous position. From there, the trader will ride the trend to what they determine as the exhaustion point and sell for a profit. Often times swing traders will utilize many different technical indicators that will allow them to have a more advantageous probability when making their trades. Shorter term traders do not necessarily tend to swing trade as they prefer holding positions throughout the day and exercising them prior to the close of the market. Swing trading strategy utilizes time and it is this time that is the deterrent factor for many day traders. Often times there are too many risks involved with the close of the market and a trader will not be willing to accept these risks.

The distinction of swing trading is a broad topic, meaning, it has many different influences from a multitude of different trading strategies. All of these trading strategies are unique and have their respective risk profiles. Swing trading can be an excellent way for a market participant to further enhance their technical analysis skills while giving them an opportunity to pay more attention to the fundamental side of trading. Many successful swing traders have been known to use a Bollinger band strategy as a tool to assist them in entering and exiting positions. Of course, for a swing trader to be successful at the strategy, they will need to have a high aptitude for determining the current market trend and placing their positions in accordance with that trend. It does a swing trader a world of good to place a short position with the plan of holding for an extended period of time in a market that is clearly trending upwards. The overall theme here is that the goal of the traders should be to increase their probability of success while limiting or eliminating risk completely. The swing trader's worst enemy is that of a sideways or inactive market. Sideways price action will stop a swing trader cold in his or her tracks as there is no prevailing trend to key off of.

When used correctly swing trading is an excellent strategy used by many traders across various different markets. It is not only used in the Forex market but it is a key tool in futures and equity markets. Swing traders take the skills that they learn through technical analysis and can even parlay these skills into various options strategies. The short-term nature of swing trading sets it apart from that of the traditional investor. Investors tend to have a longer term time horizon and are not traditionally affected by short-term price fluctuations. As always, one must remember that swing trading is only one strategy and should be utilized only when appropriately understood. Like any trading strategies swing trading can be risky and conservative strategies can turn into day trading strategies quite quickly. If you plan to employ a swing trading strategy, ensure that you fully understand the risks and develop a strategy that will be able to allow you to generate maximum percentage returns on your positions.

HOW IMPORTANT ARE EXITS
DURING TRADING

One of the things that separates successful traders from the majority of market participants is that they have a detailed plan that guides them when to close trades. For them, this is essential. It is fair to say that when a lot of traders buy shares, they have little idea of under what conditions they would consider selling. It would also be fair to say that a fair percentage of market participants routinely adopt a 'buy and hold' approach.

Whilst trading routinely involves decision making, there are no more important decisions you have to make than when to sell shares. Many traders often overlook this part of trading or underestimate how important it is.

Importantly, the outcome of every trade is dependent on the exit. If you enter in a timely manner and then exit poorly, the trade could very easily be a loss. If your entry happens to be poor but your exit is good, you might actually still salvage a profit or at the worst, minimize a loss. The exits, and not the entries, determine the outcome of your trades.

Any form of back testing will illustrate this point. You can take an entry signal but combine it with different exit strategies. You will quickly discover that you can drastically affect the overall results with only minor adjustments to the exit strategy.

It could be argued that you cannot even conclude that a particular entry signal is effective because the final results are so dependent on the exit strategy used. Bad exits can make a good entry look bad and good exits can make a bad entry look good.

Selling shares is probably the most difficult decision you will face but it is the most important. The decision is especially difficult when you are faced with a loss and all you want to do is wait for the shares to return to your buying price. The situation is made worse when the shares continue to move away from you, making your loss even greater than you would have ever imagined.

There are a number of reasons people will not sell shares when they are faced with a loss. Consider the emotions in a person who is contemplating cutting a loss. Cutting a loss means that you purchased some shares and they went down. Your initial decision to buy was wrong and selling the shares at a loss validates your mistake. Cutting your loss means accepting that you were wrong and unfortunately there are many people who cannot bring themselves to do this. Yet, it is essential.

Of the more than six billion people on earth, not one of them knows what is going to happen in the market's tomorrow or any day in the future. No one else knows, so how can you expect yourself to know for sure?

Those people who run their own business realize that they make some decisions that work out very well and others that in hindsight, were poor and perhaps resulted in losing money. However, another thing that is for certain is that they would all accept the latter as being par for the course in running a business. People who manage successful businesses would naturally accept that experiencing a loss is just a part of trading.

FOREX TRADING PSYCHOLOGY - HANDLING THE PRSSURE

You are beginning to like Forex trading. You have read every article you can find. You enjoy doing the research, developing your plan and choosing your target currencies. You are comfortable with your forex broker and his trading system. You are gaining valuable experience each day, but for some reason, you are still having difficulty pulling the trigger, perhaps more on sell signals than on buys, but the chatter in your brain is distracting. How do I deal with this kind of pressure?

First of all, let's assume that you have done the basics. You always have a defined and disciplined plan of attack when you approach any market. You do not let yourself get "emotionally married" to any position or pattern that beckons you to stick with it. And, you have learned how to manage your greed and balance it with caution, never backing yourself into a vulnerable position that is difficult to unwind. Now, what do you do?

The issue now is all about calming the mind, allowing your experiential programming to take over with the good judgment that you have developed, and then reaping the results. There have been many studies in this area, particularly with professional athletes, so why not let them be your guide.

You may get better or worse but the mental aspects of the game are a mirror image of what an individual trader must deal with in order to be successful. Coincidentally, in order to perform, an athlete or trader must be able to shift his focus from distractions and concentrate on the moment at hand.

Watch professional golfers on television, particularly when they are putting. One putt per round is all that separates them from the minor leagues, so the pressure is intense to putt well. To deal with this pressure, every Pro has developed his own personal putting routine, i.e., line up the putt, take two practice strokes, look at the cup, and then putt. They practice this routine so that it becomes second nature and requires no thought to invoke it. Then, when the real pressure is on, they do not succumb to any distraction, feelings of doubt or anxious second-guessing.

As a trader, we face similar situations that require quick and nearly automatic responses. Our emotional thoughts do affect our physiology and therefore, our ability to perform on the spot. Even neutral thoughts can be a distraction unto themselves. The more we can develop a "trading routine", the more dispassionate we can be when we have to execute a buy or sell transaction. The more practiced your routine is, the more confident you will feel. You will know with certainty what to expect, and performance will become effortless, nearly always exceeding your own high expectations.

THE NEED FOR A FOREX BUSINESS PLAN

To succeed in currency trading, it is vital to develop the best forex trading business plan. Forex stands for foreign currency exchange. The currency of one country varies from the other. Trading in currency involves selling the currency of one country and purchasing the currency of a different country simultaneously. The trading is at a rate of exchange that is agreed on for a certain period.

It is a changing market because the prices of various currencies go up and down in a few minutes. This is the reason a lot of people are investing in this kind of business. You can access this market through the internet any time and rake in profits. Losses could also be made at times. It is therefore vital to come up with a great plan in order to succeed.

A strategy helps you to approach currency trading in a systematic way. Firstly, do some research before you venture into the business. You can do this using tutorials and forex guides. You could also seek the services of experts to enable you to develop trading skills, ideas, and also to understand the business.

You may make some losses and some profits in this business just like with other businesses. Trading should thus be done with cash that you could afford to lose. You can do this by setting aside money for trading only. You could also give yourself a limit of the money you wish to spend and try to keep to this limit.

To ensure you have the best Forex trading business plan,

choose carefully the currency you wish to trade in. You

may choose popular international currencies as they are more successful in trading than others. Pair up the popular currencies. The common pairs may include USD/JPY, EUR/USD, GBP/USED and others.

Develop a trading routine and stick to it. Change it only when there is a real need. A routine includes making a decision on the time of day you will trade. Try to keep up with this routine even when the market fluctuates, as this will inculcate discipline in you and will also enable you to eventually make profits.

Have a budget to assist you in tracing your cash inflow and cash outflow. From the budget, you will identify the slump periods and peak periods of your currency trading. You should not let slumps discourage you. This means you must be patient and should avoid being emotional while trading. Do not be in a hurry to recover your losses. Instead, take time to analyze your trading strategy. This helps you to keep off any possible risks and from trading dangerously.

Your best Forex trading business plan will therefore include good management skills, discipline and patience. Trading of currency has become a source of income for lots of people. The working hours are flexible, you can work from your home and there is big potential for high income.

FOREX TRADINGPLAN

Trading is a business. As in any other business, a well-thought-out plan can make the difference between success and failure. A trading plan is a pact you make with yourself. It is your personal blueprint for success. It must include not only your goals but must also detail how you plan to achieve them. Traders work alone, and so do not need to deal with many of the organizational issues confronting other business plans. But traders need a business plan (trading plan) just as much as any other business.

The three important factors that need to be strongly engrained into our minds and ultimately into our trading plans are Trading Psychology, Discipline and a Trading System.

Trading Psychology:

Your mind is your main trading asset and must be guarded. How do you plan to protect yourself throughout your trading career? How will you guard against burnout? When and for how long will you take a vacation or a break from trading? (Remember, it's OK and it's healthy to take a break from trading). What is your plan in the event of an unusually large loss? Are there things outside your trading which heavily influence you emotionally? How do you plan to deal with them? Emotional decisions are the most destructive factor to the bottom line. Your trading plan is your protection to guard against these!

Perhaps the single most important aspect of trading and

yet the one that is paid little attention to by the average

trader, is the psychology of trading. Traders must remain emotionally detached from the market; this is easy to say but often difficult to do. A new trader will experience a gauntlet of emotions as they enter the markets for the first time - fear, anxiety, panic, joy, even greed - these are all emotions that the greenhorn trader should not only expect but be prepared to face. You need to remain emotionally detached and act according to your trading plan. Emotional imbalance impairs your ability to make intelligent decisions.

Of course, there are other things to consider besides your emotions. Do you know why you are trading? Are you trading for the thrill, for the challenge or to make a steady income? Whatever the reason, you will enjoy the experience more and trade better if you know your purpose. Many new traders approach the market with unrealistic expectations. Instead of seeing trading as a business which requires both time and some hard work, they see the market as nothing more than a place to make "quick and easy money." At first, they may do well but without any kind of plan in place invariably their inexperience and overconfidence catch up with them.

You must accept the fact that the market is always right and that at times you're going to be wrong. There is no shame in being wrong, even the best traders can be in error. If you don't admit you are wrong and do something about it, fear, greed and hope can cloud your vision of the market and can cause emotional responses harmful to your trading. Do not become in love with a losing position. If you're wrong, admit it, get out, salvage your trading capital and wait for the next trading opportunity. Conversely, congratulate yourself and feel good about a

trade when you have labored according to your trading plan, regardless of the profit or loss.

Acknowledge that you are the person responsible for your winning and losing - do not blame the market, do not blame a hot tip that did not plan out and do not blame a newsletter or financial advisor. Losses give us the chance to focus on where our plan fell short and to instantly correct it.

Discipline:

Like most things in life, you will not succeed without discipline. Discipline is adhering to your established trading plan, including entry points and stops. To become consistently profitable, we must have a high level of self-discipline with a well-defined trading strategy that effectively maximizes profitable trades and minimizes losing trades. Creating a trading plan is relatively easy but it is the discipline to follow that plan that will differentiate capable traders from all others. During periods of profit, adhering to a trading plan is comparatively easy. However, during periods of loss the same trading plan will appear rigid and constricting and it is at such times that a trader will be tempted to stray from the plan. At times you might want to deviate from your trading plan but doing so invalidates the reason for preparing it in the first place. Remember the purpose of the plan was to provide guidelines to follow. Breaking from it will often lead to risk exposure that you were originally unprepared to take.

Besides abandoning your trading plan, a lack of discipline can lead to other troubles for the trader. If you abandon your trading plan, you may be tempted to impatiently rush into or out of trades without considering the consequences. You might also start to ignore price charts

or start falling victim to your emotions. And most assuredly, you will not utilize your stop-losses. Once you ignore your stop-losses, it is only a matter of time before you make your last trade. How can you make money, if you don't have any money to trade with? The most important trading rule is to cut your losses. Even though your primary motivation is to make money and you consider this important, protecting your trading capital is even more important.

One of the best ways to manage your risk when trading is to limit how much money you put into a single position. This is to guard against the possibility of something unpleasant occurring. What is the maximum percentage of your trading capital you are prepared to commit to a single trade? If you have had three losses in a row, the likelihood that you are going to have a profitable trade doesn't automatically swing in your favor. Don't increase your trade size thinking your next winner is just around the corner. Instead, after a few losses, your trade size should be decreased slightly to reflect your reduce trading capital. You also have to ask yourself, "What happens if you keep losing money?" Are you prepared to lose all of your trading capital before you are forced to stop, or do you think you would like to hold on to some of the money and place it somewhere else, with the plan of either not trading again for an extended period of time or giving up altogether?

There is a lot to learn about managing your money in trading. Telling you to cut losses is one thing but executing it ruthlessly and without delay can be another.

Trading System:
Having a routine makes it so much easier to follow your

plan. Why is this critical? Well, why do most traders fail? Simple, they don't have a plan. A trading plan will often follow a trading routine that the trader consistently exercises over and over again. The routine should bring together most of the parts of your trading plan into a methodical and deliberate process for each and every trade.

When you do not have a written trading plan, even though you have developed a plan in your head, it is too easy to drift away and go back to old habits. Having the written plan will guide you to making the right decisions. Consider the difference between knowing what has to be done and what you want to do. In trading, what has to be done is always the right choice, yet if you do not have a trading plan, you can easily decide with what you want to do, instead.

In your routine, you'll likely be sorting through large amounts of information in the form of websites. A routine will help you manage the information flow, it is important to identify what information you need and where you will find it. What information do you really need to trade and what information is for interest only but does not affect your decisions?

Decide how you will categorize the industry/economic sectors in the market. Will you use any form of sector analysis in your method? If so, how will you use it? Will it be the starting point for your trade selection process or will it be a final filter to ensure you don't enter stocks that belong to poorly performing sectors? If you are going to use fundamental analysis, what items are of most interest to you? For example, are you interested in earnings, dividends, growth and acquisitions? If so, how will you use that information?

Write down your trading methodology. Start by talking in very general terms about how you are going to approach your trades. As examples, are you going to trade only heavily traded stocks that are trading at new 52-week highs? Or are you going to trade more speculative stocks and trade breakouts and/or chart patterns? Are you going to use technical analysis? If so, will you be looking at trends? Over what timeframe and how are you going to identify them? Are you interested in reversals of short-term or medium-term trends? If so, how will you identify them and then what will you do once you identify them? How about technical indicators? Will you use any of them? What are your conditions that you look for in all of your trades? What setups will you use and do you have printed examples in your trading plan to go back and review. Finally, what triggers will you use? Usually, following specific trading rules and keeping it simple works best!

Write down your trading methodology. Start by talking in very general terms about how you are going to approach your trades. As examples, are you going to trade only heavily traded stocks that are trading at new 52-week highs? Or are you going to trade more speculative stocks and trade breakouts and/or chart patterns? Are you going to use technical analysis? If so, will you be looking at trends? Over what time frame and how are you going to identify them? Are you interested in reversals of short-term or medium-term trends? If so, how will you identify them and then what will you do once you identify them? How about technical indicators? Will you use any of them? What are your conditions that you look for in all of your trades? What setups will you use and do you have printed examples in your trading plan to go back and review.

Finally, what triggers will you use? Usually following specific trading rules and keeping it simple works best!

It is essential that you monitor your performance for a variety of reasons. The most basic of these is to ensure you protect your trading capital. Further, monitoring your performance allows you to review your past trades and learn from your mistakes. This is an approach used by some of the best traders in the world. They will periodically review all of the trades they have conducted, both winners and losers, and learn from them. How will you go about conducting a review of your trading activities and how often will you do this? A trading diary should detail all of your trading decisions, including reasons for starting a trade, your emotions when opening the trade, trend direction, as well as daily adjustments of exits. A trading diary provides you with a methodical way of maintaining a clear focus. It can also assist you with learning from your mistake.

A written trading plan is the only way to go. It is critical that you create your plan when you are thinking clearly and then trade your plan. By planning each trade from beginning to end, you are forced to follow a disciplined and methodical approach to the markets.

TIPS TO WORK ON TRADING PREPARATION

Experts say that preparation is half the battle. In order to have a solid trading performance, you need to invest time and effort in your pre-trading routine. Here are a few tips on how you can improve your trading preparations.

Study past price action.
Before you are able to pinpoint the market themes that could affect price action for the upcoming trading days, you should first take a look at which events and issues have been influencing movement so far. This can help you form your biases, on which you can base your next trades.

Read up on market events.
After establishing which themes have been moving the markets so far, it's time to figure out whether there will be potential changes or not. Economic calendars provide a bird's eye view on the events that could impact price action for the week so you should do your homework and find out if these releases could spark trend continuations or potential reversals.

Mark the inflection points.
Being aware of prevailing market themes and potential changes from upcoming events can help you determine what kind of trade setups you will take. If you think that trends will continue, you can look at whether the trend lines line up with possible support or resistance levels. If

you believe that a reversal will happen, you can also look at nearby support or resistance levels from which price may bounce.

Psych yourself up!

After doing your review and research, you still have to prepare yourself mentally and emotionally for the trading week ahead. To do so, you can come up with your own routine or ritual to boost your confidence and get you in the zone. Some do this by playing upbeat songs or by downing a cup of coffee to be extra alert.

Come up with exit strategies.

Before you actually take any trades, remind yourself that there is always a chance that your analysis may be wrong or that a surprise market event could completely change the outlook for price action. For these instances, you should always have an exit plan in place that you will be ready to execute. This will help eliminate the fear or panic involved when you see that price isn't behaving the way you expected it to.

These are just some of the many ways in which you can improve on your trade preparations. Constant discipline and motivation are necessary in order to be fully prepared for the trading battle.

MONEY MANAGEMENT AND TRADING

Many people believe that most day traders lose money and only a few are profitable. While this view has some merit, the difference between successful day traders and unsuccessful day traders often has its roots in money management technique. In referring to money management, it should be clear that talking about money management is a reference that relates to your futures account balance.

One skill that is universally prevalent in unsuccessful traders is inferior money management skills. And for the record, it is a well-known fact that discussing money management is very unpopular among traders; it is generally assumed, for unknown reasons, that traders understand proper money management as it relates to trading. Nothing could be farther from the truth, especially for a trader with a smaller account.

Many brokerages tend to lower their day trading margin requirements, especially in recent months as the volatility in the market has subsided. One futures brokerage that has lowered its day trading ES margins to $300 per contract. While this may be, at face value, very appealing to the average day trader, it is not convincing that this trend is such a great idea. Lowering margin requirements is often an enticement to traders to trade more contracts in their account, and hence end up taking on more risk than is acceptable. Since the mini futures contracts are highly leveraged, trading more contracts than general money management techniques warrant could lead to massive losses and unacceptable losses. Overextending your risk

tolerance model is a quick way to exit the futures trading business.

So how many contracts should you trade?

Let's consider an example: Trader A establishes a futures trading account with $3500 as his initial margin balance. Further, he saw the ad on the Internet with the brokerage firm offering $300-day trading margin requirements and quickly signed up with the firm. Every brokerage has a risk management department and they assign him a maximum contract limit of five contracts. Let's assume Trader A is a bracket trader and sets his stop-loss at 12 ticks. Trader A is excited about the possibility of trading 5 contracts. Let's calculate what he is risking on this particular trade. On the ES contract, each tick is worth $12.50. So, $12.50 x 12 = $150. With his plan to trade 5 contracts, he is risking $750 (5 contracts x $150). In this example, Trader A is risking approximately 22% of his account balance on this trade. This is nearly 22% of his entire margin account. Obviously, Trader A is far overextended in the number of contracts he traded. This behavior is not unusual.

How many contracts should Trader A be trading?

Proper money management technique would dictate that day trader risk 5-7% of his total account balance on a given trade. One would even grant that an aggressive trader might be justified in risking up to 10% of his account balance on a given trade. At 2 contracts, Trader A would be risking $300 or just under 10% of his account balance, which is an acceptable level of risk for an experienced trader. A novice trader should probably only trade 1 contact on any given trade. Either 1 or 2 contracts keeps a trader well within a normal risk tolerance model. Anything more than 2 contracts are excessive and exposes the trader to unacceptable levels of risk. At 5 contracts, a trader could easily be out of money with 4 unsuccessful trades.

Money management is really about managing risk. A wise trader does not expose himself to excessive risk and potential financial ruination. Day trading is not a get rich quick proposition and one secret to success is managing your money properly. Learning to trade the number of contracts that correlate to your futures account balance is an important skill to learn. All too often, traders over trade their account through poor money management implementation.

Making the grade in the futures trading game requires employing consistent money management technique and a trader who employs poor money management technique will likely squander his potential profits and, in the end, his entire trading account. Keep your potential financial risk under 10% on all trades and you stand a great chance of staying in the game.

HOW TO IMPLEMENT MONEY MANAGEMENT STRATEGIES

Most people getting started in the foreign exchange business focus all their attention in learning a good Forex strategy, method or system. Most of them think that if they become able to make profitable trades, they will become profitable traders and eventually trade Forex for a living. That's where most traders are completely wrong!

A Forex strategy, method or system it's just an instrument to determine when a price or market conditions offer a good investment opportunity. The way we manage money is what determines if we'll get rich or go broke trading those opportunities

So, as you can see, having a good Forex money management system is extremely important.

But what exactly is money management?

Money Management can be a strategy or system to move money from a place to another minimizing loses and maximizing profits.

Many people think that defining their risk to 2-3% per trade and calculate the distance for the stop loss and the pip value in every trade, is money management.

And yes, this is an important part of a money management strategy but there is a lot more in it.

So, how can we manage money correctly?

The Broker:

That's the first step to take in consideration to manage money in Forex.

Most retail traders can afford to invest 1-5k in their business, some of them even less than 1k. Although high leverage gives us the chance to buy/sell large amounts of money with a small margin deposit, not every broker allows micro accounts where a trader could buy 1K lots instead of the mini 10K and standard 100K lots.

Some brokers even support lots of 100 units of base currency, very few like will allow you to buy single units.

Micro accounts are better because they allow traders to distribute risk equitably avoiding the asymmetrical leverage, which is deadly dangerous for traders.

Fixed $ Amount in drawdowns:

This money management strategy is helpful for recouping quickly from losses, the trader will trade a % of the account when successful but will trade a fixed amount when an unsuccessful trade hits: e.g.

10.000$ 2% risk = 200$ RR= 2:1 GAIN= 400$

10.400$ 2% risk = 208$ RR= 2:1 GAIN= 416$

10.816$ 2% risk = 216$ RR= 2:1 LOSS= 216$

10.600$ FIXED A= 216$ RR= 2:1 LOSS= 216$

10.384$ FIXED A= 216$ RR= 2:1 GAIN= 432$

10.816$ 2% risk = 216$ RR= 2:1 GAIN= 432$

11.248$ 2% risk = 224$ and so on...

It takes you only one trade to recoup completely from two losses.

Compounding
Compounding is a very powerful long-term money management strategy. Basically, reinvesting the gains of each successful trade and avoid making withdrawals for a relatively long period of time will boost your account like you never imagined!

Separated capitals
This concept allows a more aggressive trading approach. The trader split his total trading capital in two: one for risk and one for safe.

The risk account is the 5% of the total trading capital and the 95% is in a separated safe account. The trader will only trade with the risk account (5% of total trading capital) but will risk 15-20% of the risk account. Each time he doubles the account, he recalculates the 5% of the total invested capital and re-split the money equitably in the two accounts.

Implementing one of those Forex money management strategies or mixing a few of them will allow you to maximize profits and minimize losses the best way possible.

Fixed Fractional Money Management
Trading totally at random with a 50% winning percentage and an R multiple of 1 yields no advantage, as one naturally expects. Remember that an R multiple is the average win

divided by the average loss. Such a system poses neither an

advantage nor disadvantage. The average outcome should come out extremely close to the starting balance.

Most traders focus on risking a set dollar amount such as $1,000 on a given trade. Fixed fractional money management updates that dollar figure after every single trade. It changes the overall outcome after you add up all the winners and all the losers. Remember that trading is the net outcome of several hundred trades or even thousands of trades. The power of a position sizing or betting strategy comes into play as the number of trades increases.

Fixed fractional money management stretches some portions of the bell curve and compresses other regions. Before we get into that, it's important to remember what fixed fractional money management means. It stands for the idea of risking a set percentage of the current account equity rather than the starting equity.

Consider an example where the account balance starts at $100,000 risking 1%. Both methods risk the same amount on the first trade, $1,000. The next trade however, will yield a different risk amount. A win on the previous trade would increase the account equity to $101,000. One percent of a 101 grand is $1,010 of risk on the next trade. A whopping ten-dollar change.

That may seem trivial. It is most certainly not over the long run.

Examples

Consider a trader that plays a coin toss game and has a system with the following characteristics:

He starts with a $100, 000 account balance

His R multiple is 1.0

He wins 50% of the time with no trading costs

He risks 1%

A flip of heads means that he wins. He loses when the coin lands on tails.

The absolute worst outcome of playing the coin toss with a fixed dollar risk of $1,000 is a loss of $46,000. Adding fixed fractional money management during that difficult drawdown improves the drawdown to a less substantial loss of $37,500. The worst drawdown goes from -46% to - 37.5%. The method drags the absolute worst-case scenario and pulls it closer to the average. When an unlucky, devastating drawdown kicks in, the technique reduces the losses that the trader experiences.

The best-case scenario for fixed dollar risk is a $58,000 (58%) return. Adding money management to the system dramatically stretches the best-case scenario further to the right. It improves to a $76,000 return (76%). The good times get a lot better without changing anything at all about the trading system. The method stretches positive returns away from the average. The trader walks away with more money in his pocket.

The natural instinct is to conclude that fixed fractional money management is the way to go. It improves the risk reward profile of a totally random strategy. Adding it to a real trading system should help control parameters that most traders consider critical like drawdowns and maximizing the return.

An important consequence of using fixed fractional money management however, is that the odds of receiving a below average return increase somewhat. The coin toss game suffered a below average return, 47% of the time. Applying fixed fractional money management increased the likelihood of a below average return to 53%. The effect is not all that much. Losing is more likely. But when it

happens, the "loss" is so negligible that it can be thought of as breaking even.

Random numbers occasionally follow a seemingly non-random pattern such as loss-win-loss-win. When this occurs, the size of the trade on the losses is bigger than the trade size of the winners. Even if the winning percentage comes out at precisely 50%, those wins get slightly overshadowed by the losers. That micro effect of slightly larger losses than gains shows up as a slightly increased risk of not making as much money as expected.

Graphing all outcomes

Red areas represent the losing outcomes while green areas represent the winners. Money management is really about maximizing the ratio of green area to red area. Random trades with no expectation of profit yield a standard bell curve.

Fixed fractional money management moves the highest density of returns slightly to the left. Doing so creates the trivial disadvantage of a slightly increased risk of negligible loss. Importantly, the far-left side (the worst case loser) gets dragged much closer to the average. The far-right side (the best case winner), gets stretched much further from the average. The tradeoff is a slightly increased risk of loss in exchange for better extreme outcomes.

MONEY MANAGEMENT-HOW MUCH TO RISK PER TRADE

It's a sad fact that 90% of beginner Forex traders blow up their trading accounts in their first month of trading. The surprising thing is, this happens regardless of whether they have a profitable Forex trading system or not! Clearly, there's more to making money in Forex trading than having a profitable Forex trading system. What most beginner Forex traders don't realize is that when you're just getting started in Forex, having a good Forex money management strategy is far more important than having a system with huge returns. By the end of this article, you'll know how to apply the best Forex money management strategies for consistent, safe returns from your system.

Even if you have the worst Forex trading system in the world, you won't blow up your trading account if you have a good Forex money management strategy. On the other hand, without a good Forex money management strategy, you could have the best Forex trading system in the world and it wouldn't even matter. That's how important money management in Forex is!

You need to understand how important it is to protect your capital when you're trading Forex. Unfortunately, most beginner Forex traders start out with too little capital. They try to turn $1,000 into $100,000 by being extremely aggressive and risking a big chunk of their capital on their trades, and when the inevitable loser comes along their account take a huge hit. It's like taking two steps forward and three steps backwards every couple of days: frustrating and unsustainable in the long-term.

Believe it or not, the best Forex money management strategy is to dial your risk per trade way down to between 2-4% of your capital. This is the best cutting-edge Forex money management strategy that all the big banks and hedge funds apply for all their traders and it is highly recommend that you apply it as well. It's called the % Capital Strategy and it provides the optimum growth of your trading account with almost zero risk of blowing up your trading account entirely.

An Example of Good Money Management in Forex
Here's how it works. If you're really conservative, go with 2%, and if you're really aggressive, go with 4%. Any higher or lower and you're literally throwing money away. For an account size of $10,000, using a conservative setting of 2%, your maximum risk per trade would be $200. That means that if you have a stop 20 pips away from your entry, then you're allowed to take a maximum of 1 full contract.

A key decision that you need to make early on is whether you want to re-invest your profits or not. Obviously, re-investing your profits will allow you to leverage the power of compounding returns, while withdrawing your profits will not. By re-investing your profits, you can literally double or even triple your profits in a year! If you decide to re-invest your profits, then you'll have to update your risk per trade allocation and your position sizes at regular intervals. An advice is to update your position sizes every 5-10 trades, so that you're getting the best compound growth of your trading account.

It's important to remember that you're still going to need a proven, profitable Forex trading system to make a

consistent Forex income. Even the best Forex money management strategy will not make a bad trading system profitable, but without a good Forex money management strategy it's impossible to make a lasting Forex income. Be sure to have both of these two essential Forex trading elements in place and you can be sure of your Forex trading success!

BENEFITS OF MONEY MANAGEMENT

The benefits of having good money skills when it comes to money management are incredible. Being able to effectively manage your money will open up new avenues in your life that were previously unavailable due to a lack of money. Learning how to manage your money will essentially give the disposable income that is required to live a life without limits. Few other skills compare to that of effective money management.

Live a More Stress-Free Life

When you manage your money correctly, you should live a more stress-free life. Money is one of the most stressful things in someone's life and therefore has to be managed properly to reduce the stress involved with it. Effective money management will avoid some of the serious consequences that come with not staying up to date with your bills, sending your kids to college and any other type of stress that money brings to one's life. If you always have some spare cash lying around, you will feel much more secure. The security that money brings plays a huge part in helping people to reduce stress.

Achieve Your Dreams

Everyone has different dreams in life. However, almost every dream that one can have involves money in some way or another. Being able to effectively manage money is the only way for most people to achieve their dreams if they do in fact involve a financial component. You are not going to be able to take your partner on that dream

vacation without money. That is just not how the world works. However, if you effectively manage your income then that dream vacations becomes a lot more realistic. Having money can help you achieve all sorts of dreams besides vacations as well. You may dream of sending your child to college or seeing your favorite professional sports team in live action. Either way, chances are your dreams will cost you money and money management can be the path that gets you to making those dreams really happen.

Travel and Take More Vacations

While a dream vacation may not be in your plans, you will probably agree that you would like to be able to travel more. Traveling and seeing the world is something that costs a lot of money. For most people, having good money skills is their only hope of being able to travel and see the world. There is a reason that most all people with money choose to spend it on traveling the world and seeing all that earth has to offer with their own eyes.

Enjoy Ultimate Freedom

Sadly, in this world, money affects the amount of freedom a person has in their day to day life. If you have unlimited money, then you can literally do almost anything you want. You can sleep in, eat out, go to the moon and almost anything if you have the right amount of money. By attaining some great money skills when it comes to money management, you can continuously open up your life to more freedom.

PLATFORM AND TOOLS FOR TRADING FOREX

Online Courses

Online courses may not be considered a tool for trading to most people, but they are available and beginners are encouraged to utilize as many as possible. These courses are designed for beginners, so they often use simpler language and introduce terms that new investors need to be aware of. They are also a great resource for those that are just starting out and would like to find some tips to help them get started and to help make sure that they do not lose all of their money. Investopedia is a great source for beginner traders.

A Broker

Every person that is interested in the market needs an online broker. This is the person that will take your money and then bring it to the market, making trades and things of that nature. When looking for a broker, make sure to take into account any commission that they will receive and their previous experience. Beginners may want to take the time to interview a few different brokers to guarantee that they wind up with an online broker that is perfect for them.

Automated Software

This may not be a necessity, but it is definitely at the top of the list of forex tools. Most automated software will complete trades for people, making it easier than ever before. These programs will help the most inexperienced person come out on top of the market, they run by themselves and they can be turned off, meaning that they will only make trades when the consumer wants them to, and when the program is running.

FX Calendar

A calendar of events is important for every trader. This calendar will mark important dates in the market, such as when economic results are released. The economy is the market and it can easily mean a huge gain or a huge loss. To prevent a huge loss, an individual need to be aware of what is going on in the market and when, to pull their money out or throw more money in. One of these is one of the best tools and most of them are free.

Notifications

Receiving notifications may not be free, especially for those that do not get text messaging for free but it will be well worth it. Investors can set up notifications to see when there are important changes in the market. This fx trading tool is especially useful for those that are interested in the market but are always on the go.

Time Zone Convertor

Typing "what time is it in Japan" is effective, but this can get tiresome after so many times of typing it. A time zone convertor can often be downloaded for free and can easily tell traders what time it is in some of the most important cities that pertain to the market, such as New York, New York, United States.

Forex trading can be confusing to some but these tools are going to help with the most basic things. They are great ways to get started, as beginners continue to explore the wonderful world of fx trading. Other tools are available to make estimating the perfect day to make a move easier than ever in addition to other wonderful products, such as special calculators. If there is something about the market that is confusing, there is a tool to help with it.

The availability of excellent tools for online currency Forex trading has enabled retail Forex (foreign exchange) traders to operate on a level playing field with professionals in the interbank trading marketplace. Necessary tools include a retail trading platform, which can be run on either a windows PC, or a web browser (potentially non-Windows) or on a mobile device, including Smartphone, Blackberry etc.

In recent times online forex broker companies have been able to use internet connectivity to develop a community of small investor, retail forex traders. Instantaneous price and deal information, at one time restricted to banks' private networks, is now available to the private retail forex trader, via his PC or mobile.

Private individuals can now access the Forex market rapidly and effectively, using retail trading platforms. This allows fair competition ("level playing field") with dealers in banks and financial institutions. There are a number of types of retail trading platform. These include windows PC platforms, browser and web-based solutions and platforms designed for mobile devices.

Traditionally, the widest range of features would be found in a windows PC platform, which would be installed on the trader's laptop or PC. Some users though, may prefer a web

based or browser-based solution. The user would in this case be able to log into his account from any PC with a web browser and internet connection. This would allow the use of non-Windows PC's such as Linux and Macs, and would also allow more flexibility of access, for example when traveling.

Also, there are retail Forex trading platforms which run on mobile devices such as palm and pocket PCs, Smartphones and Blackberry. These would usually have a less comprehensive set of features that a Windows based platform but would of course allow the user to make deals from any location with a mobile phone signal.

When trading in Forex markets, there is always the possibility of loss as well as gain. Traders need to be aware of the concepts of risk, leverage and margin, and should only be trading with risk capital, which they can afford to lose without drastic effects on their lifestyle.

In common with nearly all specialist software applications, stock trading tools have exploded in number and in their capabilities since the early 1990s. What exactly are these tools and which are the best ones for you?

Trading platforms and other stockbroker services

These are arguably the tools that have evolved the most quickly and to the greatest extent. Even the original, basic platforms that first appeared in the late 1990s were revolutionary compared to the system we had before - using the telephone to instruct your broker. Now with the latest developments, you can enter, amend or close a trade with just a few mouse clicks and it's almost (though not quite, of course) foolproof, with prices being displayed automatically, different colors for buying and selling, etc.

Apart from the trading platform, the main service that such sites provide is up to the minute news and news feeders. Now, you have at your disposal all the instant news that the internet provides, all the information bearing on your trading that you could desire. Unless you are a strict technical analyst taking no notice of news or other events that may influence future price movements then you need constantly updated financial and market news.

Charts and indicators

These have evolved beyond all recognition as well. Most brokers and many websites not linked directly to any individual broker, have charting services available which invariably include a host of indicators that are customizable to your requirements or those of your trading system.

Now charts are available on any stock, index, commodity, bond or currency traded on any financial market and in most cases they can go back for ten years or more. In seconds, you can load your own simple moving average settings or any other indicator or combination of indicators onto them.

Online educational resources

Most stockbrokers have their own customized training available to their customers. It's unwise to rely too much on any such package but nonetheless, it is often possible to learn a great deal from these resources. My own preference is for independent coaching from an experienced and successful trader, rather than a broker. You have available online video, DVD video as well as audio and the more basic eBooks, none of which was available to any degree before about 2003.

One most important and significant development is that of the "demo account". This is without doubt a major breakthrough and valuable asset of the trader, both new and experienced. This account enables you to test strategies and techniques in real time to see if they really work, without risking real money. There's a temptation to trade recklessly precisely because it's not real money, but my advice is always to treat is as real money if you really want to learn and to have reliable results, whether good or bad.

Trading robots

These are the latest tools to arrive on the financial trading scene. Pioneered in the forex market, they are beginning to establish themselves as mainstream stock trade software. In theory, you set your parameters, e.g. how much of your capital to risk on any one trade, stop loss levels and load your chosen indicators or "expert advisors". The robot will open and close your trades for you, taking away the human emotional element that so often leads to losing trades.

At the present time, they don't seem to be able to take into account the fact that market prices are influenced by humans, with all our emotional baggage. But there's nothing to say they can't evolve and improve. In the meantime, if you're tempted to buy one, test it out thoroughly with a demo account before risking real money with it.

STOP LOSSES

A Stop Loss order is placed to protect the trader from losing more money on a trade than they are willing to risk. A trader opens a position either long or short a trading vehicle. At the same time, the smart trader will enter a Stop Loss order opposite the opening trade. If the first order was a buy, the Stop Loss will be a sell order for the same number of units. This helps to keep emotion out of a trade or making it a hope trade. "I hope it quits losing me money soon" is a hope trade. Do Not Begin Trading without an order to protect your capital. Hope trades are for amateurs and will cause only losses, be it in the stock market, the futures market or the currency market.

Although many traders do not use this method of trading, the traders that do use them are more likely to be winning traders in the long run. They have analyzed the trade and have a very good idea of how much risk they are willing to accept as part of the trade. If the trade goes against them, the Stop Loss will protect the capital and keep the loss at an acceptable level. Without an order in place, the trader has to manually get out of the position by putting in an order to close the position. This is where the good trader and the lucky trader part company. The good trader controls losses and the lucky trader just depends on being able to move when he is forced to move. This is where the trade can turn into a hope trade and the trader lets emotion control the trade rather than logic. This is the easiest way to turn a small loss into a big loss. Do not be a fool and trade without Stop Loss orders.

Placing Stop Loss orders is an art form and there are considerations to be made. One is where to place it, perhaps at the level in which the trader first entered into the trade. Traders might prefer a trailing stop loss to protect a profitable trade. The trailing stop could be used as the trade makes money. Entering new orders and canceling the old order at the same time makes this a trailing stop. This can also be used as a way to further protect a profitable trade by closing up the current price level and the stop order price. Eventually, the order will be triggered but the profit may be greater than just getting out of the trade by feel. As with all trading, the idea is to use as little risk as possible and still give the trade some breathing room.

Stop Loss orders should be used at entry and then later to keep as much of the profit as possible. These are two very distinct and different uses of this valuable order. It means lower losses and more possible profit.

Remember that Forex Trading involves substantial risk as well as a chance for substantial profit. Protect yourself with Stop Losses and other tools at your disposal and trade wisely.

RISK OF BEING UNDERCPITALIZED IN FOREX TRADING

One of the biggest causes of failure in automated Forex trading is not having enough capital to begin trading with. It's easy to be sucked in by claims that so and so turned a hundred dollars into ten thousand dollars in just a couple of months but the reality is that, aside from a huge amount of luck, there's really no way that anyone can actually do that in real life. You need a significant amount of starting capital to begin trading properly, in addition to a healthy attitude towards minimizing risk. Here's what you need to know to keep yourself out of trouble.

The Best Money Management Practice for Automated Forex

In automated Forex trading, it's extremely important that you understand the right application of money management and risk management before you even turn on your system. That's because this is a key parameter in the operation of any system and normally, the default money management settings given to you will be too risky. With high rewards come high risk after all, and the developer would have ramped up the risk to create the big numbers on the sales brochure to entice you to buy.

Contrary to what most traders think they know, the key to success in Forex trading isn't how much money you make, but how much money you keep. To retain the maximum amount of profits and protect your capital at the same time, the first thing you need to do is start with enough money. Every Forex broker account has a minimum lot size and every system has a minimum risk, and you need to be sure that your starting capital is enough to cover both these amounts. Otherwise, you're risking more than you have to and that will almost certainly blow up your account.

Automated Forex Money Management Rule of Thumb

Here is a money management rule of thumb that is used in automated Forex system trading. First of all, you calculate the maximum possible loss in pips that your system can have. Next, you multiply that figure with the minimum position in dollar value that your broker allows you to take in any given trade. The figure you get is the maximum possible loss in dollars that you can possibly have. The rule of thumb is that you should only risk a maximum of 2% of your capital in any given trade, so to get the minimum starting capital you need for your automated Forex system, all you do is multiply your worst possible dollar loss by 50 and you have your figure.

Sticking to the 1% Rule of Trading

Career day traders use a risk-management method called the 1-percent risk rule or vary it slightly to fit their trading methods. Adherence to the rule keeps capital losses to a minimum when a trader has an off day or experiences harsh market conditions, while still allowing for great monthly returns or income. The 1-percent risk rule makes sense for many reasons, and you can benefit from understanding and using it as part of your trading strategy. *The 1-Percent Risk Rule*

Following the rule means you never risk more than 1 percent of your account value on a single trade. That doesn't mean that if you have a $30,000 trading account, you can only buy $300 worth of stock, which would be 1 percent of $30,000.

You can use all of your capital on a single trade or even more if you utilize leverage. Implementing the 1-percent risk rule means you take risk management steps so that you prevent losses of more than 1 percent on any single trade.

No one wins every trade and the 1-percent risk rule helps protect a trader's capital from declining significantly in unfavorable situations. If you risk 1 percent of your current account balance on each trade, you would need to lose 100 trades in a row to wipe out your account. If novice traders followed the 1-percent rule, many more of them would make it successfully through their first trading year.

Risking 1 percent or less per trade may seem like a small amount to some people, but it can still provide great returns. If you risk 1 percent, you should also set your profit goal or expectation on each successful trade to 1.5 percent to 2 percent or more. When making several trades a day, gaining a few percentage points on your account each day is entirely possible, even if you only win half of your trades.

Applying the Rule
By risking 1 percent of your account on a single trade, you can make a trade which gives you a 2-percent return on your account, even though the market only moved a fraction of a percent. Similarly, you can risk 1 percent of your account even if the price typically moves 5 percent or 0.5 percent. You can achieve this by using targets and stop-

loss orders.

You can use the rule to day trade stocks or other markets such as futures or forex. Assume you want to buy a stock at $15, and you have a $30,000 account. You look at the chart and see the price recently put in a short-term swing low at $14.90.

You place a stop-loss order at $14.89, one cent below the recent low price. Once you have identified your stop-loss location, you can calculate how many shares to buy while risking no more than 1 percent of your account.

Your account risk equates to 1 percent of $30,000, or $300. Your trade risk equals $0.11, calculated as the difference between your stock buy price and stop loss price.

Divide your account risk by your trade risk to get the proper position size: $300 / $0.11 = 2,727 shares. Round this down to 2,700, and this shows how many shares you can buy in this trade without exposing yourself to losses of more than 1 percent of your account. Note that 2,700 shares at $15 cost $40,500, which exceeds the value of your $30,000 account balance. Therefore, you need leverage of at least 2:1 to make this trade.

If the stock price hits your stop-loss, you will lose about 1 percent of your capital or close to $300 in this case. But if the price moves higher and you sell your shares at $15.22, you make almost 2 percent on your money, or close to

$600 (fewer commissions). This is because your position is calibrated to make or lose almost 1 percent for each $0.11 the price moves. If you exit at $15.33, you make almost 3 percent on the trade, even though the price only moved about 2 percent.

This method allows you to adapt trades to all types of market conditions, whether volatile or sedate and still make money. The method also applies to all markets. Before trading, you should be aware of slippage where you're unable to get out at the stop loss price and could take a bigger loss than expected.

Percentage Variations

Traders with trading accounts of less than $100,000 commonly use the 1 percent rule. While 1 percent offers more safety, once you're consistently profitable, some traders use a 2 percent risk rule, risking 2 percent of their account value per trade. A middle ground would be only risking 1.5 percent or any other percentage below 2 percent.

For accounts over $100,000, many traders risk less than 1 percent. For example, they may risk as little as 0.5 percent or even 0.1 percent on a large account. While short-term trading, it becomes difficult to risk even 1 percent because the position sizes get so big. Each trader finds a percentage they feel comfortable with and that suits the liquidity of the market in which they trade. Whichever percentage you choose, keep it below 2 percent.

Withstanding Losses

The 1-percent rule can be tweaked to suit each trader's account size and market. Set a percentage you feel comfortable risking, and then calculate your position size for each trade according to the entry price and stop loss.

Following the 1-percent rule means you can withstand a long string of losses. Assuming you have larger winning trades than losers, you'll find your capital doesn't drop very quickly but can rise rather quickly. Before risking any money—even 1 percent—practice your strategy in a demo account and work to make consistent profits before investing your actual capital.

CAPITAL PROTECTION

The $5.1 trillion foreign exchange marketplace is a great place to be – high liquidity and profit potential that surpass those of other market segments. But being a trader can be risky in a volatile and unpredictable market.

Unfavorable trading conditions can hit you when you least expect it and regulatory requirements may adversely affect your operations. Many traders are unsure where to turn as security and integrity of their deposits has seemingly become a luxury.

Until recently, you may have overlooked the benefits of working with a financial custodian.

What is a Custodian? A custodian is a financial institution that holds customers' financial assets (e.g. money) for safekeeping, in order to minimize the risk of their theft or loss.

For brokers, fund managers and individuals seeking deposit protection against the risk of their broker becoming insolvent and only getting back cents on the dollar, we strongly recommend opening a custodial account (through a Tri-Party contract agreement). Essentially, a custodial account is a financial escrow account established in the client's name and administered by a responsible person or entity, known as a custodian, who has a fiduciary obligation to the beneficiary.

What are the benefits of having a tripartite agreement?
Safeguarding from unforeseen events – the
agreement adds protection to the money of the account

holder in the unanticipated event that their broker
becomes insolvent.

Real separation of customers' funds – all client equity is secure and fully segregated at all times in the client's name and the client funds are not co-mingled with the broker's funds or those of any other client. The money is held by an independent custodian company or bank, who administers the assets for the protection of the client.

Added service worth – security of funds is a primary concern to clients, especially in light of recent events. More and more clients are choosing to work with the institutions offering the maximum security for the funds on deposit in their accounts such as Custodian accounts, insurance on their deposit, segregation of client funds and others.

Traders and investors can access this type of service. This financial service provider places a strong emphasis on trust and transparency in the broker-trader relationship while fully understanding your trading needs. They seek to resolve pain points experienced by traders, such as:

- Lack of previous experience or knowledge of the new broker you are to trade with.
- No existing feedback/reviews of the broker on the Web.
- The possibility of having your profits withheld.
- The possibility of a broker "going dark" on you.
- The possibility of a brokerage going bankrupt, leading to capital losses.
- Involvement of high risks when sending money overseas to unknown recipients.
- Broker manipulation of trading accounts.

While custodians are nothing new, by entering the retail Forex space, they anticipate that long-established conflict of interest between traders and brokers will be eliminated by the solutions provided. Custodian services allow all traders (investors) to benefit from:

- Risk protection over unpredictable events
- Actual funds segregation
- Maximum funds security

Traders (end-users) can enjoy the benefit of having their deposits protected by a custodian knowing that their funds are truly segregated. This engenders a level of trust between brokers and traders. There is then more accountability and transparency, reducing the anxiety that both parties exhibit when it comes to talking about transactions, disbursements and compliance procedures.

PROTECTING YOUR TRADING CAPITAL

More than 90% of people trading the share market lose money and the major reason is because the majority do not use correct Money & Risk Management principles: Money Management, Position or Trade Sizing. No matter what you call it, You Better Know It!

"Money Management is like sex: Everyone does it, one way or the other but not many like to talk about it and some do it better than others. However, there's a big difference: Sex sites on the web proliferate, while sites devoted to the science of Money & Risk Management are somewhat difficult to find." - Gibbons Burke

NEVER risk any more than 2% of Trading Capital on any one trade.

e.g. If you have $30,000, your maximum risk is $600 but what many forget is to also cater for brokerage. If it's say:

$25 each way your maximum risk is now $550 and a stop is set appropriately so if your share drops in value by $550 you exit.

Never Trade with more than 20% of Trading Capital on any trade.

e.g. Again, if you have $30K your trade size would be $6000 but its preferred to use 19%. So, if I have 5 open trades and will still have 5% of my trading capital out of the market to allow for things like slippage, education, data, etc.

Here is a simple mistake many make in relation to Trading Capital?

e.g. The trade, using the above example, is now worth

$7000 up to $1000, so I decide to open my second trade. The correct method is to first determine the share value if current trailing/profit stop is hit. You may be up $1000 but your trailing stop is set and if hit, you make less, say $900, so the next calculation would be based on $30,000 + $900. "The only things in life that are certain is Death and Taxes!" Benjamin Franklin

So it should be noted that past performance is not a reliable indicator of future performance but you can control the risk.

It's the 21st century and it's quite normal to manage one's own investments, yet very few implement disciplined, professional money risk management principles or understand them. During the stock market boom, limiting risk was always an afterthought but given the recent volatility & market conditions, get serious!

Professional Money and Risk Management strategies, used correctly and in conjunction, will be your foundation to trading success. Essentially, Money Management tells you how many shares to trade at any given time and Stop placement is where you must accept you have made the wrong decision, close that trade and move on. It is a defensive concept that keeps you in the game to play another day. Don't confuse Money Management with Stop placement. Stop placement does not address the question of "how much"?

Risk Management is the difference between success and failure when trading shares. It refers to Stop placement and will minimize any losses and you will have them but also maximize any profits and this stop is called a Trailing, Maintenance or Profit Stop.

Money Management optimizes capital usage. Few have the ability to view their portfolios as a whole. Even fewer traders and investors make the move from a defensive or

reactive view of risk, in which they measure risk to avoid losses, to an offensive or proactive posture in which risks are actively managed for a more efficient use of capital.

PROTECTING POSITIONS BY HEDGING

Forex hedging is hedging in the Forex market. Hedging involves a trader plummeting his/her risk in trading. This does not get rid of the risk or the injuries caused by an unforeseen occasion in the market that causes the place of the trader to unfavorably have an effect on his/her money, but good hedging can decrease the unenthusiastic result on those finances. There are some positive fundamentals that any Forex investor must be acquainted with about, and it is these easy and bottom main beliefs that will construct the basics of capability when they grown-up with the market. Essential values of Forex let investors, counting promising and new investors from further markets, to appreciate its dynamics and completely understand the risks concerned when dealing in paper trade. It is only from side to side that the realization that their decisions and strategies can grow up sufficiently, so that they are clever to plan approximately market psychology and create cash from the market.

The word Forex hedge would denote nothing to you if you are new with Forex trading or the Forex market, as with additional workings of trading and strategy with the paper trade. Investors use this word as a means to reduce their risks in reading. Forex hedging is a defensive strategy, a security net that they put approximately on their investments to diminish the risks and maybe even add to their odds of survivability in the market. Most citizens would explain Forex hedging as a kind of indemnity diagram against investments, which means that you are

insuring the cash you are putting into the market. But is there a price?

Well yes. Initially, it is not completely full evidence and does not provide you full reporting. Hedging will defend your investments to a convinced degree and when something terrible occurs in the market, probability of you finishing off enhanced than your peers who have opted not to hedge would be considerably far above the ground. Fundamentally, if you're in trading, you will have the alternative to hedge but more highly, can study to do so. In relation to big multi-billion-dollar corporations to minuscule person traders, hedging is fairly lengthily skillful. Characteristically, they do this by offsetting any price-related risk by means of market instruments and the easiest technique of doing this is to hedge one asset next to another.

More often than not the major investors do this by investing in two unlike things with unhelpful relations. The price for Forex hedging is attractive far above the ground and from time to time, investors sense it does not actually deserve make use of, some sense that the money payment gained is worth it. As you can observe, there are two sides to this site and frequently, hedging is avoided by promising investors as it concerned the use of derivatives and is fairly complex in natural world. Central banks, government, finance institutions and only the additional experienced investors use hedging to defend their investments, which can frequently run into millions and even hundreds of millions of dollars.

For the informal investor, hedging is not an alternative just yet, though some may sense that in these unsure times, it is a first-class design to assure their investments and come out secure from even the most horrible hit situations. Keep in mind whenever you hedge, that the intention of it is not to create cash but to defend what you previously have to a positive degree. Consider the pros and cons, and how much you have invested, then the choice to hedge will come much easier.

It is best to understand that hedging does come at a value - you have to disburse for the hedges, in spite of whether you wanted them or not. You have to create certain that the hedges are value the cash that you will use on them, particularly if the predictable unenthusiastic consequence does not occur. If you can't give good reason for the money you will use on the hedge, then you must not hedge your chief investment.

In addition, Forex hedging in itself will not build you money; it is there to assist defend your finances from unfavorable and unforeseen proceedings that would cause your main investments to lose money. You require to be convinced that the hedge will defend you as well as you believe it will. Those who are inexpert or who are not completely conscious of how hedging mechanism works, might think that they are secluded to a big degree by a hedge he/she executes, then discover after an unfavorable occasion that the hedge didn't defend them as predicted or at all. This can result in overwhelming losses from the most important investment AND the price of the hedge as well.

Implementing good Forex hedging can be an effectual instrument for the well-informed trader. Appropriate hedging can get rid of much of the danger and monetary losses that traders can encounter when unpleasant and unforeseen world events cause the currency hedging principles to vary in habits that are not predictable. By learning how and when to hedge, you can add to your probability of being winning of trading on the Forex market.

BASIC TIPS ON HEDGING

What Is Forex Hedging?
The easiest way to understand hedging is to think of it as insurance. When you hedge, you are insuring yourself against a negative event. This does not mean that once you hedge the negative event will not happen, but instead, if it does happen the impact of the event is reduced. An example is like getting a car insurance.

With Forex hedging, you are essentially placing a bet in both directions of the market. You are placing a buy and a sell order on the currency pairs. This allows you to hedge your bet to reduce your risk in the Forex market and potentially profit from movement in either direction. This requires training and if done properly, it is a good skill to have as a Forex trader.

In Forex hedging, there are essentially a few types of hedging strategies

- Buy and sell the same currency pair, same lot in the almost the same timing. After some time, one order will gain while the other will lose. When the winner run out of steam, take profit and wait for the losing trade to turn around. This strategy works well in a yo-yo kind of market trend.

Example: Buy 1 lot EUR/USD at 1.3400 and sell 1 lot EUR/USD at 1.3397. If the price goes up to 1.3460 and we close the order to take 60 pips while the sell order has a drawdown of 63 pips. In such market condition, the rate will start to fall. If the rate fall to 1.3420 and you close the sell order with a loss of 23 pips. Overall, we have gain 60 pips - 23 pips = 37 pips. Experience trader typically use technical analysis skills to decide their entry and exit points.

However, such strategy is no longer allowed if you have a broker that adheres to National Futures Association (NFA) rules. If you sign up with a FOREX broker that is not in the NFA, you can still employ such hedging strategy in your account. For those that still wish to use hedging, there are a number of ways to do so.

- Hedging with correlated pairs

Use currency pairs that have strong correlation. In other words, there are currencies that mirror each other as they move. The move can be directly or inversely proportional to each other. For example, if you look at charts of EUR/USD and USD/CHF pairs, you'll find very close similarity in the graph patterns. This means that traders can use this similarity in moves to try to reduce losses and built a hedging strategy that could combine these two currency pairs. Since EUR/USD and USD/CHF move inversely, one can BUY both pairs. The result will be one order will gain profit and another will lose. Thus, they will cancel each other. Hence, one can work out a profitable hedge strategy similar to item 1.

- There are also other forms of hedging being employed, such as Hedging arbitrage - This technique involves getting 2 brokers. One charge interest and one do not. Buy from the broker that the currency pair provides you rollover interest and sell from the broker that does not

charge rollover interest. This way, you can gain the interest or SWAP that is credited to your account. Be careful not to get margin call, so managing the two accounts by transferring money from one account to another is crucial so that you have enough fund in both of them.

Pros and Cons of Hedging

Hedging can be very important when the market is highly volatile as it can be used to substantially reduce the risk levels. Hedge is also used to allow a trader to stay in a seemingly bad trade much longer, allowing for the market to correct back in the trader's desired direction. At the point that the hedging position is taken any existing loss is locked in, so if the trade never recovers, the trader will eventually need to take that loss. The good part is that you do not need to make that decision right away, thus give the market some room to move. If prices move back in your favor, the hedge position can be closed and the original trade now move in favor of your intended direction.

However, note that no strategy is fool proof and as such Forex hedging will not provide full coverage. Hedging will protect your investments to a certain degree and when something bad occurs in the market, chances of you ending off better is higher than other traders who have opted not to hedge. When you decide to hedge, you must remember that it comes with a cost. You should make sure that the benefits you get from a hedge should be more than enough to make it worth your while. You should make sure the expense is justified. If it is not, then you should not hedge. The goal of hedging is mainly not to make large gains but instead it is used to protect your losses.

Forex hedging is actually a protective strategy. It is typically not recommended for newbie. In manual trading, it is very important that you have a clear understanding of Forex hedging before you decide to use it as insurance. You need to ensure that you actually need it and the benefits you get from hedging are adequate enough to make it worth your while.

MONEY MANAGEMENT SECRET

Did you know that you can lose huge sums of money trading Forex, even if you have a profitable Forex trading system? Contrary to what most Forex traders believe, a profitable Forex trading system is not the be all and end all of successfully trading Forex. The secret to keeping your trading account safe and growing your returns exponentially at the same time is the little-known practice of Forex trading money management.

What Is Forex Trading Money Management?

Forex trading money management is basically how much you should risk on each trade and there are many different money management strategies out there. One popular example that you will hear about often is the 2% rule, which states that you should not risk more than 2% of your trading capital on any one trade. Most people get confused with this definition because they confuse margin with risk per trade, so I'll explain it in a different way: if you're using the 2% rule, then you should size your positions in such a way that you will not lose more than 2% of your capital in any given trade. For example, if your stop is 10 pips away and 2% of your capital is $200, then you should only take 2 contracts (2 Contracts x $10 per pip x 10 pips = $200 risk per trade)

The Limitations Of Traditional Forex Trading Money Management

Most people follow the 2% rule religiously without knowing

why they are meant to do it. I personally believe in

knowing why I'm doing something before I do it, so researched this thoroughly. Turns out that if you want to minimize the risk of blowing your trading account while maximizing your trading profits in the long run, then you'll want to keep your risk per trade to between 2-4 % of your trading capital. Depending on your own tolerance for risk, you can actually go up to 3% or even 4% to ramp up your profits even further, without greatly increasing your risks.

The Secret Exponential Money Management Method
The 2-4% Forex trading money management model is a type of geometric money management technique and is the most efficient way of growing your capital when trading Forex. Traditionally, people apply Forex trading money management using a fixed contract sizes, which is good for small accounts but not very efficient. The reason the 2-4% rule is so powerful is because it allows you to apply the power of compounding to your trading. As you gain profits, you reinvest it over and over again, which creates an exponential growth rate in your trading account. I'm sure you'll agree that when it comes to your trading profits, an exponential increase is far better than a linear increase.

The Power Of The 2-4% Rule
There are two ways of applying the 2-4% rule. One is to update your position sizes at the end of regular time intervals, and the other is to update your position sizes at specific profit/loss milestones. Regardless of which method you apply, it's clear that the 2-4% rule is powerful because it creates the fastest and safest growth of your trading account. Obviously, you will need a profitable Forex trading

system to apply this Forex trading money management

strategy successfully. Once you have these two components in place, then there's really nothing stopping you from creating a consistent Forex passive income that grows over time!

CREATING STREAMS OF PASSIVE AND ACTIVE INCOME BY TRADING

When you first start looking into trading as a profession, there are a lot of different markets to consider: commodities, futures, Forex, options, ETFs, stocks, etc. Because there are so many different products out there to trade, it's hard to decide where to start! But before diving in headfirst, let's identify a few basic principles.

First, you'll need to determine how much money you would need to make trading as a full-time business - and rest assured, trading is a business - because this number will be different for everybody.

That means figuring out how much money you need to make to cover your expenses. The easiest way to figure out your overhead cost is to break down how much money you need to make each month and day, then calculate the minimum amount of money you need total.

After calculating overhead, you will then need to map out a strategy for trading to reach your goal. Passive investing and active trading are two of the most common ways to approach the stock market. It's infinitely up for debate which one is "better" or "safer", but in the end, it comes down to which investment strategy is right for you.

Many investment companies outperform their competitors by actively trading versus passive investing, when done correctly. However, if an active trader isn't investing with discipline, he could easily lead himself into huge losses. For this reason and many more, many professional traders seek stability in trading both passively and actively as a collective strategy.

In fact, one of the most lucrative benefits of the trading business is the potential to generate both active and passive income. Active investing entails short-term buy and sell signals. Active investing also involves trend following or if you're both really good and lucky, grasping market anomaly opportunities.

A day trader, for example, is someone who holds positions for a very short time and makes numerous trades each day. This could mean an excess of $200, $500 or even $1,000 in active income being generated by the trades daily and that money can be taken out of your account the very next day. Wouldn't it be nice to get paid on a daily basis?

On the other hand, trades can go for days, weeks or even months without any further involvement and passive income is then accrued in your brokerage account. Passive investing, also known more traditionally as "buy and hold", is a process in which assets like stocks and mutual fund shares are acquired for the long term, either through diversification or selective asset picking.

Essentially, buy and hold passive income is like having employees or other companies constantly at work for you. The combination of active and passive trading ensures multiple streams of income and allows at-home traders much more freedom than a traditional business.

So, what are some of the reasons people get into trading? There are many: perhaps the desire to create financial freedom, need for the ability to step away from their current job or maybe even vacation more often. Day traders are usually freer to spend more time with friends and family than what traditional employment can offer.

But to be able to accomplish your goals (whether they match those mentioned above or are something different altogether), multiple streams of income, both monthly and daily income though active and passive trading is necessary.

For some people, the means to this end are entirely different kinds of investment vehicles; real estate would be a great example, though the popularity of trading speaks for itself. Consider that while thousands of high-profile investors have found real estate to be a great vehicle for financial freedom, stocks and options provides the invaluable advantage of near instantaneous liquidity of assets. This is one of the biggest attractions for any successful investor, regardless of the vehicle.

But remember, we're only at step one. We need to break down how much money you'll be required to reserve on a daily and monthly basis so you can determine if this business is going to be a viable option for you and your family as you start up.

You've made a great choice in deciding that trading for active and passive income is the right business move for yourself and stocks, options, and other open, public financial markets are a great way to get there.

GENERATING PASSIVE INCOME THROUGH FOREX TRADING

Forex Signals

Forex signals are short messages that can help new traders to decide on which currencies to trade and when. They can be sent via text message, email or any other form of communication. You'll also often find them on social media websites like Twitter, FX forums and on some of the leading Forex trading platforms.

A Forex signal is usually a short piece of information which instructs the user to take an action. This could be something like BUY USD/EUR @ $1.16700 or SL @ $1.12000. Sometimes Forex signals will also feature a type of order such as LO (limit order), PO (pending order) or MO (market order).

There are a lot of websites online that will teach you how to read these signals and how to understand them. Forex signals can also be free or premium with the latter tending to lead to better trades. That said, there are a lot of Forex signals providers who will happily send this information to people in order to bolster their reputation in the industry. If you don't have the time to learn how to trade Forex, or you simply want to do so in the easiest way possible, Forex signals may be a good option for you.   It is, however, important to perform some research into the Forex signals providers to avoid losing money. Approach the signals with caution and you could make a good passive income.

Forex Robots

Perhaps the most passive way of making an income from Forex is through the use of Forex robots. These perform automated trades on your behalf, so you literally don't have to do anything once you have set them up (although it is still wise to keep an eye on the trades being made on your behalf).

In order to get started, you will need to perform some research into the software available. You want to choose one that meets your needs and that you can rely on to perform your trades correctly. When you have this setup, the computer program (Forex robot) will make trades based on predetermined Forex signals. It will use its knowledge to decide to sell or buy at a specific time, gaining you money in the process.

Though almost all Forex robots claim to be able to make you money, this isn't always the case. A computer program can be wrong in the same way that a human being can. A lot of Forex robots are also scams, which is why some of the leading news platforms like Forbes and the Wall Street Journal refuse to promote them. This is especially true when the robots are free. Checking out reviews and testimonials before trusting your money to an automated program is a good idea.

Thankfully, websites like InvestinGoal.com are available which review the various platforms out there. For example, they've recently published a review on the platform FxPro which gives an honest opinion and outlines the numerous pros and cons. You also get a detailed analysis of how it works and how you can get started on it, which is helpful for any newbie. Forex robot is a feature of FxPro, so this may be a worthwhile option to go with.

Social Trading

Social trading works in a similar way to a social network. However, instead of sharing videos of cats and pictures of their lunch, social traders share information on the trades they are making enabling others to copy them. In order to make money from this kind of trading, new traders just need to find a trader that they trust and then copy their trades. During the process, they won't just make money, they'll also learn how, why and when a good trader makes their moves, giving them more insight into the industry.

The hardest part of social trading is finding somebody to copy that you can trust. Once you've done some research into the different platforms and found someone you can work with, you can get started.

In some cases, you will need to pay a small commission to any trader whose trades you copy. However, this amount is usually negligible and not something most new traders worry about when making a passive income.

Forex trading is something that a lot of people have considered getting into, but many don't know where to start. The above three options are all ideal for beginners with each requiring a different time investment. Just make sure to do your research before choosing a platform and getting started.

MONEY MANAGEMENT STRATEGY

Money Management Strategy 1: Martingale
You can ask any gambler around and believe me, they know what this strategy is about like they would know their ABC's. The idea is straightforward and simple: as you lose more, you increase your risk. For example, if you risk $50 and lose, you need to bet $100 on the next turn. If that doesn't quite work, bet $200. After a long enough losing streak, theoretically and statistically, you will win. And, if you have doubled your risk right from the onset, that single win could recoup your initial loses and if you are fortunate enough, even gain some profit.

The question however, is this: do you have enough to finally win and make it back? Unless you have an unlimited amount of money to spend, this is hardly a reliable strategy. There are a lot of newbie Forex traders who adopt this strategy. Unsurprisingly, it leads not only to great losses but much worse, to wipe-outs!

Money Management Strategy 2: Anti-Martingale
The anti-Martingale is the opposite of the above money management strategy. The idea is to increase your risk when you are winning and tone it down when you are losing. Like the Martingale strategy, this is high-risk, but it's perfect for traders who want higher returns while still keeping their initial balance. There are many experienced Forex traders who adopt this money management strategies, and with good results!

Money Management Strategy 3: One Percent Risk Rule

This system has saved many traders from total bankruptcy and wipeouts. The beauty in this strategy is that it's simple and effective. The name says it all: for every trade, you should adjust your risk to roughly 1 percent of your account's balance. Here's an example: let's say your account has $1,000,000. One percent of it is equal to $10,000. That means your Stop Loss should be tweaked so that, for every trade you go into, you will not lose more than $10,000. Simple and effective indeed but why is it that only a handful of traders adopt this? The answer is that they are not looking for moderate profits. They want to hit it big in as little time as possible.

MONEY MANAGEMENT-KEY TO BIGGER GAINS

Money management is the difference between making stellar gains or wiping your account out. Here are some important points to keep in mind when adding it to your Forex trading strategy.

Risk & Reward

Risk goes with reward and this is common knowledge. Yet, many traders try to restrict risk so much that they actually create it and ensure they lose.

For example, day traders think their taking small risks as their stops are close but their 100% guaranteed to lose over time because all short-term volatility is random.

The risk looks small but the odds are stacked against them. Another example of trying to restrict risk too much is trailing a stop to close and getting stopped out by normal volatility then sees the trader get stopped out too soon. These traders need to make a study of standard deviation of price part of their Forex education.

Betting to Win

Just like the successful card player, you need to load up your bets on high odd hands and fold losers quickly. When you have a high odds trade denoted by your Forex trading system, up your bet size.

You hear many traders bang on about risking 2% per trade but this is ridiculous for most traders.

For example on a $10,000 account, that's $200! How close would your stop have to be?

To close and guarantee you are stopped out by volatility.

If you want to win, bet 10 - 20% on your high odds trades.

Stop placement

In Forex trading, most traders like to trade with stops behind support and resistance and you will notice, on many occasions, how many times a price spikes through the stop in the day and then closes below it.

If you can always use a "stop close", this will prevent from daily volatility hitting your stop in the day session or if you can't keep an eye on the market use "at or in the money options."

Trailing a stop

If you are long-term trend following, you need to give the market plenty of room to breathe and keep your stop back. Don't jack it up after a day or so like most traders do - leave it alone. When you have good profits, move it behind key support, at a 40-day moving average penetrated on a close basis which works well.

If you want to follow long-term trends, you are going to have to accept that you will give a lot back at the turning point but if you get 60% of the major trends, you will do well.

Targets

I find stop trailing hard and like to work with a target and get out when its hit.

If the move carries on, so what? I am happy as I got what
I want.

In shorter term, swing trading targets are essential as these smaller profits can disappear quickly.

How you deal with risk, will be the difference between you losing or winning at Forex trading. Try and restrict risk too much and you will guarantee you lose but take meaningful risks at the RIGHT time, with courage and conviction and you could enjoy fantastic currency trading success.

Remember the old gamblers saying:

"There's a time to hold them, a time to fold them and a time to get out of town fast"

It's very applicable to forex trading and money management!

www.ingramcontent.com/pod-product-compliance
Lightning Source LLC
Chambersburg PA
CBHW072136170526
45158CB00004BA/1402